CW00377279

AGAINST ELITISM

JASON VICK

Copyright Jason Vick 2020

"Do you know where the power lies? And who

pulls the strings?" Rancid, "The 11 Hour."

"Political theory might be defined as a tradition of discourse concerned about the present being and well-being of collectivities. It is primarily a civic and secondarily an academic activity."

"In recent years, American society has grown more inegalitarian, more divided by extremes of wealth and poverty and of education and ignorance, more openly ruled by elites, more systematically dominated by corporate power, more retarded by a mass media that ensures political and cultural immaturity, and in its politics, more systematically corrupted by money."

Sheldon Wolin, *The Presence of the Past*, pp. 1 and 207.

Preface

Elitism concerns both those on the left and the right. As the following pages argue, ordinary citizens in the United States (and many other countries) are engaging in a justified, long-overdue rebellion against political, economic, and intellectual elites.

It is my hope that this short book can contribute to the cause of greater democracy and less elitism. Though I write from the left, there is much in here that ought to appeal to all Americans who would like to see ordinary citizens have more power over their federal government, state governments, cities, towns, neighborhoods, schools, universities, workplaces, and other aspects of their lives.

In the following pages I draw on scholarship, journalism, and personal experience to make this case. It is not comprehensive but it is a start.

I say this with all seriousness. Power to the people!

A Note on coronavirus and expertise
Listen to public health experts! This suggestion is consistent with the perspective advocated here. As I recognize throughout this text, there are real experts, i.e. people with genuine specialized knowledge, from biology and chemistry to history and political science.

What do not exist are experts on the fundamental political questions—what kind of government is best? How much inequality is acceptable? What rights exist? Who gets to make decisions? What kind of laws should we pass? These fundamental political questions can only be decided democratically, through discussion and contestation in the public sphere.

In the case of the coronavirus, public health experts can tell us how to avoid disease transmission and how to quarantine effectively, while nurses and doctors can use their expertise to save lives. These are deeply important and we should defer to them. They cannot tell us, however, how to cope as a society with these challenges.

What kind of economic stimulus should we pass? Who should benefit? How do we weigh the costs and benefits of various policies? Is a universal $1000 check to everyone better or a series

of tax cuts? How about a progressive universal income that increases in value for those who
are poor? Should key industries be nationalized?
Given loans? Should student debt be forgiven?
Even economists cannot give us "expert" advice
on some of these questions, for many policies inevitably benefit some groups and harm others.
There is no expert answer for how to adjudicate
between such claims. They must be decided by all
of us democratically.

So, the perspective advocated here argues that our
system is dominated by political and economic
elites who have frequently not acted in the interest of the vast majority of people, focusing instead
on preserving their own political power and economic privilege.
To be against elitism, and for greater democracy,
is to be for better, more effective, government.
In emergency situations, like the unfolding coronavirus threat, it is more important than ever
to listen to the deeply informed advice of public
health experts.

In the long-term, a more democratic society, informed by expert advice but run by the people,
will better serve our interests than a system dominated by a small share of political and economic
elites. These elites are not experts but rather
powerful self-interested actors, and they do us
harm when they rule in our stead.

CHAPTER ONE: INTRODUCTION

This is a story about elites, the small number of political, economic, and intellectual figures who wield enormous influence and power. It is also a story about elitism, the worldview that justifies rule by elites and criticizes democracy (rule by the people). It is necessarily a story about politics.

Politics is about power. Who gets what resources, which decisions are made, who even gets to make those decisions. In the past five to ten years there has been a rebellion on a massive scale as citizens have elected populist outsider candidates and voted against establishment candidates and parties. Brexit, President Trump, the Sanders' candidacy, the shrinking and disappearance of center-left and some center-right parties in Europe; these are all related to a global rebellion against elites and elitism.

Put simply, elitism is a worldview that justifies rule by elites and is hostile to democracy. Elites are the political, economic, and intellectual people who wield disproportionate power and propagate the elitist worldview. This book shows that the intellectual arguments in favor of elitism are not persuasive and that elite rule, in practice, consistently produces devastating outcomes for ordinary citizens, particularly those in the working class.

What should replace elite rule and the elitist worldview that justifies it? A populist, participatory vision of democracy, in which ordinary citizens have more political and economic power. The problems with the elitist worldview and the elite rule that it is built upon are explored more fully in the following pages, with a focus on trade, inequality, knowledge, and the university system.

The fundamental thesis of the book is this: elites dominate our politics, economy, and intellectual life and rely on elitism as the worldview that justifies this. In practice this has produced devastating consequences for the vast majority of people in America and therefore a more egalitarian, participatory form of democracy is the solution.

I focus on elitism because it is impossible to make sense of American (and global) politics today without understanding elite rule, the elitist worldview that underlies it, and the ongoing rebellion against these very elites. There is a widespread (and justified) cynicism toward elites today—this project helps to direct that frustration toward the actual elites who have done so much damage: economic elites on Wall Street and in the extractive industries, corporate lawyers and lobbyists writing trade agreements, political elites in both parties who answer to these interests at the expense of the working class, and intellectual elites in universities and think tanks providing evidence and arguments in favor of elite rule and corporate dominance.

This book covers real-world examples of elite incompetence but just as importantly shows that *intellectual arguments* for elitism are misguided. It is not just that elites living in self-enclosed bubbles and perpetuating their economic and political dominance is bad; it is also the case that the ideological scaffolding that justifies their power is bad. There are no good reasons for elite dominance. The following chapters, by focusing on four key areas (trade, inequality, knowledge, and the academy), demonstrate examples of elite incompetence and the flawed arguments put forth to justify this elite power. This in turn provides a defense of democracy, even if at first glance it does not appear to.

This is because elitism and democracy are intertwined. They stand at opposite sides of a spectrum. Pull in one direction, you pull away from the other. It is therefore not surprising that defenses of democracy are often built around critiques of elitism and vice versa.

I am deeply sympathetic to democracy, with "its irreducibly populist strain" and deeply skeptical of elitists, both liberal and conservative, who disdain or cast a wary eye towards populisms.[1] One could build a library constructed solely of books warning about populism, from the early modern period to the present. This book shares the assessment made by political theorist Sheldon Wolin that "the dominant forms of power in the society, both public and private, are inherently antidemocratic in their structure and objectives and that if democracy is to be practiced and extended, the conditions of politics will have to be transformed."[2] In this book I build on these twin assumptions: our current institutions are not very democratic, not very effective, *and* that it would be salutary for them to become much more democratic. I thus criticize many political and economic institutions because they are *not democratic enough*.

I also take to heart Wolin's admonition that political theory, with its concern for fundamental questions of justice, freedom, and so on, is "primarily a civic" activity and not an esoteric academic one. Ordinary citizens can and do engage in it.

We can now flesh out the basic thesis of this book in more detail: Elitism as a worldview that consists of intellectual criticisms of democracy, the people, and popular rule is wrong. Elite rule, that carries out these principles, is destructive for the vast majority of people and often deeply incompetent even in achieving its own professed goals. In other words, elitism as a worldview and set of practices is responsible for many key problems in the world today. The answer is more political, economic, and intellectual democracy. A more participatory democracy is both a good in itself and will likely produce better outcomes, judged on the basis of how they serve the vast majority of citizens.

Before moving on a little clarity is in order. What do I mean by elitism? This term has many meanings; in this book I will focus on *political* elitism. Political elitism refers to the set of ideas, discourses, and practices built on the following assumption: there are specific forms of true political knowledge and objectively true answers to political questions that are akin to other forms of scientific knowledge. This knowledge, like all forms of scientific knowledge, is possessed by a select, educated few. This educated few should, and likely will, have more political influence than the ignorant masses. Elitism in this form thus resembles a sliding scale: the less true political knowledge you have, the less political power you should have. This idea can be traced back to Plato's *Republic*, in which he famously suggests that his ideal city should be governed by a carefully vetted and highly trained class of philosopher kings.

Some thinkers, like political scientists Christopher Achen and Larry Bartels, do not advocate for reducing the formal political power of the citizenry but are nevertheless best described as elitists. This is because they share the general assumptions stated above and direct the focus of their research, as I discuss in chapter four, to the ignorance and follies of the citizenry. In other words, like all elitists dating back to Plato, they suggest, implicitly and explicitly, that the problems with a democratic political system are to be found in the people. This elitist worldview is seen more widely through thousands of pages of elitist texts and speeches attempting to demonstrate this point. The elitist authors of these texts also tend to avoid any discussion of elite malfeasance or recognition of the fact that the "ignorant" masses do not make policy in a direct or indirect sense.

Thus, while some elitists like Plato (or Jason Brennan, today) are openly contemptuous of democracy, others are willing to accept or even defend representative forms of democracy, like Joseph Schumpeter and more recently Christopher Achen and Larry Bartels. The latter thinkers nevertheless want to place strict bounds on the power of the people and regularly deride their ignorance and incapacity for genuine rule. These are therefore elitist defenses of representative democracy; that is, they defend representative democracy in part because it limits the power of the people to directly rule and they oppose attempts to expand citizen participation in decision-making.[3] Joseph Schumpeter went so far as to suggest that after an election citizens should not be allowed to contact their elected representatives.[4] This would reduce "the political nature of the new citizen" by confining it "to periodic elections once every two, four, or six years."[5]

Political elitism thus exists on a spectrum, ranging from total opposition to democracy (Plato, famously ranking democracy as the second worst form of government) to grudging acceptance, or even celebration, of the limited democracy allowed in representative systems (The Federalist Papers, Schumpeter, Achen and Bartels). In both cases, political elitists oppose efforts to institute *participatory and direct democracy*. Many contemporary defenses of representative democracy, as well as those offered by the authors of the Federalist Papers in the 1780s, are republican in nature. That is, they believe democracy to be one, but only one, important part of a mixed political system that will ideally also contain aristocratic and even monarchic elements. They oppose *pure* democracy, like that found in Ancient Athens, and expect the American republic to curb the "excesses of democracy."[6]

In short, there are two predominant elitist perspectives on politics. They are distinct but related. One says, in effect, that the United States has enough democracy—to further democratize the system would be folly. This view, grounded in classical republican political thinking, sees democracy as one component of a good government that must be tempered through the wisdom of elites and institutional checks and balances that will inhibit majority rule. The second view, in effect, says that any amount of democracy is too much and that we should roll back even the limited amount of democracy we currently have. Among classic political theorists, Aristotle represents an early version of the former perspective and Plato the latter.

I reject both of these assumptions in their entirety. As I discuss throughout the book, we should reject the assumption that the political sphere is akin to an academic discipline. Politics is not political science. Political scientists may possess specialized social scientific knowledge regarding courts, public opinion, party formation, and so on. They do not, however, have specialized knowledge of the political, as a sphere of human activity, because it does not admit of such knowledge. The political is the aspect of human interaction that concerns the general interest and the common good—what matters to all of us. The only way to answer such questions is for all of us, intersubjectively, to come together and work out the answers. They cannot be found in philosophy or science. The political sphere is the sphere in which there are no ready-made answers.[7]

Contra Plato and today's elitists, neither abstract philosophy nor empirical science can supply us with answers to questions like: What is justice? What is freedom? How should resources be distributed in our society? How should collective decision-making be organized and who should be allowed to participate? In what form? What *kind* of goods and services should our society produce? What behaviors should we encourage? Which should we discourage or prohibit, if any?

"The task of the citizen is to insist upon widened debate in these vital matters: to reclaim public space as a space for deliberation, criticism, and alternatives and to prevent important political matters from being depoliticized and turned into in-house discussions." Wolin hits the nail on the head here, for it is a key desire of elites and the worldview of elitism to reduce major political questions to elite-driven, technocratic, "in-house discussions."[8] Discussions, in other words, that only experts are capable of participating in.

The understanding of the political sphere advocated here thus inevitably leads to a democratic perspective. I take democracy in its most literal sense, to mean rule by the people. Demos = people, kratia = rule. What does this look like in practice? The answer to that question has varied over history but one thing is clear: for a genuine democracy to exist the people must rule in a more direct and ongoing sense than voting in elections every few years. Representative democracy is thus an important, but only partial, step, in the direction of more democracy. This vision of democracy, in which the people rule in a more direct and active fashion, has sometimes been called participatory democracy and this is the term I will use here, although it could lose the adjective. Genuine rule by the people is *inherently* participatory.

This participatory perspective must be preserved "as an ideal form, the measuring rod of what it means to be a citizen...democracy stands for an alternative conception of politics," one that is opposed to predominant modes of elite-dominated political and economic power. A participatory democratic perspective is troubled by the current state of affairs, in which "the pervasive presence of the state, the rise of technocratic elitism, the closely knit structure of state and corporate bureaucracies, and the decline of the ideology of egalitarianism in favor of meritocracy" lead to a situation where "democracy primarily serves a rhetorical function with little or no correlative in official institutions or practices."[9]

Finally, in terms of definitions, we must discuss the elites. Elitism is a worldview, an ethos. It is a series of words as well as institutional and policy prescriptions for how the world ought to be. It can be embraced by anyone, though elites are its most prominent advocates.

So who exactly are these elites? Discussion of "elites" often invokes eye-rolling and accusations of conspiratorial thinking, so let's be clear what we mean. Elites in America, and in most countries today, consist of the following:

Economic elites: CEOs, CFOs, corporate board members, corporate lawyers, other high-level executives in big business, hedge fund managers, major stock holders, investors, and other various individuals who are largely though not exclusively found in Wall Street, Silicon Valley, the extractive industries, and media conglomerates, to name a few sites. They also include various lobbying organizations for big business.

Political elites: Senators, Governors, US House representatives, high level staffers, strategists, donors, judges, lobbyists, policy and other advisors, party organizers, and upper echelon executive staff at the state and federal level, as well as influential media figures (including in television, radio, and print).

Intellectual elites: faculty and high-ranking administrators at the most conventionally prestigious universities, heads of think tanks and their most politically connected researchers, op-ed writers and other highly visible journalists and commentators, large publishing houses, newspapers, television pundits, editors of prestigious academic journals as well as pundits with radio shows that have millions of listeners.

These are real people with inordinate influence and power. They overlap heavily. The economic elites literally represent less than one percent of the population and many can accurately be described as oligarchs. Although some of the political and intellectual elites are in this economic one percent, some are not. Nevertheless, the political and intellectual elite are invariably found in the broader professional classes, which constitute the most educated and highly paid twenty percent or so of Americans. Even the modestly paid elites earn far more than the median American households, which must get by on annual incomes between $50,000 - $60,000.

As I discuss in more detail elsewhere, there are good reasons to be committed to a populist, participatory vision of democracy. This would include, in part, making workplaces, universities, and NGOs, not to mention cities, states, and the federal government, more democratic through various institutional reforms. In practice this will mean that citizens have a more direct say on budgets, investment, work, parks, development, educational priorities, and many more things than they currently do. This is a goal and a demand but it is not an end state. Democracy is a radical demand regarding the future, not a conservative accomplishment regarding the past.

In the real world there will always be problems with democratic institutions and there will always be pushback from elites trying to capture or eliminate democratic practices and structures. Democracy therefore exists on a spectrum, in which we can have more or less. It does not exist as a simple yes or no question, as social scientists and pundits sometimes insist. According to the perspective offered here, the answer to the question "do we want more democracy?" is going to almost invariably be "yes." But this does not mean that democracy is perfect, whether for a workplace, a neighborhood, or a national government. The best we can say for democracy is that it is better than the other forms of government and making a polity more democratic will, all things equal, be a positive step towards a better world.

This book discusses democracy and elitism in the context of four areas: trade (and the economy more broadly), inequality (political and economic), knowledge (public versus expert), and in the academy. It demonstrates that in each area elitism as a worldview offers a flawed assessment of the real world and elite rule produces destructive consequences for the poor and working class. In each case the book argues that America would benefit from more democracy and a more democratic outlook in place of elitism.

In practice this will require more democracy in

our neighborhoods, cities, states, and federal government, as well as in workplaces, boardrooms, banks, and universities.

This is not a definitive account but a brief foray into a large world of ideas and political contestation. When it comes to the political world, I side with the demos, for they are the citizens who constitute our democracies. I am one of them.

CHAPTER TWO: RETHINKING TRADE

In recent years the global trade regime and the particular deals that help comprise it have come under growing criticism, not just from the citizenry but from major political figures seeking the Presidency. In 2016, for instance, Bernie Sanders, Donald Trump, and, belatedly, Hilary Clinton all came to publicly oppose the proposed Trans-Pacific Partnership (T.P.P.) then being negotiated under President Obama. All three claimed that, if elected, they would withdraw from the agreement. Once elected, President Trump did in fact do this.

Yet, the T.P.P. was in many respects similar to NAFTA and other recent trade deals considered by the US. It was broadly supported by senior leadership in both political parties, intellectual elites in the think tank and policy world, and economic elites. It was also relatively unpopular with the broader public but this is no surprise: NAFTA was deeply unpopular in the 1990s. The difference is that in 2016 certain influential political figures were defying the claims of powerful elites and siding with the broader public. Why is this? What changed? In this chapter I tackle this question and try to lend a little insight into how we might productively rethink trade in a manner more attuned to the interests of the working class and less to the interests of global elites.

This is a story about what happens when elites make trade policy. It is also a story of how we might move toward a world where this is no longer the case.

I want to begin by identifying three broad perspectives on global trade. These are ideal types, pitched at a general level. Real thinkers and actors may not perfectly correspond to these categories. They are still useful for thinking through these issues:

1) Global trade is unequivocally good
2) Global trade is good in aggregate but creates winners and losers. The winners must therefore compensate the losers to ensure that the results are fair.
3) Global trade, as it has been practiced in recent decades, is actually bad for most people.

A disclaimer: I am not arguing against trade per se but against the global trade regime as it has been practiced in recent decades, in a manner that is designed by and largely serves the interests of global corporations at the expense of ordinary workers. The global trade regime includes the structure of the WTO (World Trade Organization), its rules for membership and enforcement, bilateral and multilateral trade deals such as NAFTA, and permanent normal trade relations with China. In Europe the trade regime includes rules for European Union members and requirements for those countries that use the Euro (the Eurozone). I am in favor of trade that is designed with the interests of the many in mind, a point I will elaborate below.

Perspective 1 represents what used to be called the Washington Consensus, i.e. the perspective that was dominant in both American political parties, major think tanks, among pundits, book publishing houses and newspapers, Wall Street, Silicon Valley, other economic elites, lobbying organizations, as well as much of academia (particularly economics but not limited to this discipline), and other thought leaders and elites, including the individually wealthy, from the 1970s until probably the great recession. (We could say it reigned for about 30 years, from the late 1970s to the late 2000s). This perspective, which in its semi-sophisticated guise, draws on the economic work of Adam Smith and David Ricardo, argues that more trade is good because it leads to specialization and therefore each nation producing on the basis of their comparative advantage.

In other words, totally free global trade will lead each country to produce the goods and services that it is most efficient at producing. Free trade kills off our unproductive industries and replaces them with ones that we are better at (and does the same in every country). This is because other countries that can produce a good more efficiently than us will provide it for less, we will buy the cheaper product, and our less efficient, and thus more expensive industry, will collapse. Every country therefore produces what it is most efficient at, and worldwide wealth is maximized. This story has at least some truth, in that reduced trade barriers often (though not always) lead to higher global GDP.[10]

From this theoretical position followed the completely unjustified next step, that if global trade is good, any and every specific trade deal proposed, whether global, multilateral, or bilateral, is also good. This was exemplified most explicitly when *New York Times* columnist Thomas Friedman noted that he supports all trade deals without even reading them, on the basis of the above arguments. Although Friedman was unusually blunt, his position was the same as most of the elites mentioned above: unequivocal embrace of any and all deals referred to under the name of "free trade."

How could such ideas be so uncritically embraced by political, economic, and intellectual elites? One answer is that these ideas were a part of the ideological world that elites resided in. Just as fish don't sense that they are swimming in water, so these elites did not recognize the neoliberal worldview, which seeks to extend market rationality to all aspects of life, that they were swimming in.[11] Neoliberalism is a concept that frustrates both those in the center and on the right, particularly because it is hard to isolate as a measurable variable. It is a worldview, actively propagated by some and tacitly embraced by others, that has grown in prominence and influence since the 1970s. It is effectively summarized by Luke Savage in the following terms:

"But neoliberalism also variously describes: an existing set of interconnected economic and political institutions; a conscious ideological offensive that transformed global politics in the 1980s and '90s and the frontiers of acceptable public policy since; a range of principles that guide elected leaders of both the Right and the liberal center whether they are conscious adherents to neoliberal philosophy or not; and the near-totalizing reality of life under the pressures and logics of late capitalism."[12]

This full-throated, unequivocal embrace of any and all trade became hard to sustain and take seriously after the recession and increasing scholarship and advocacy regarding the negative impact automation and trade were having on working classes in the US, Canada, and Europe, particularly with regard to massive increases in inequality and the disappearance of good middle and working class jobs.

So it was replaced, arguably, with perspective 2, which we could now consider the main consensus, held by both parties, many pundits, and economic and intellectual elites. This position, which seemed something of a radical challenge to the Washington consensus in the 1990s, is now the mainstream position: global trade is good in the aggregate but it creates both winners and losers. The winners must compensate the losers through higher taxes, job retraining, and other forms of social insurance.

This perspective, at its left edge, leads some, like prominent economists Joseph Stiglitz and Thomas Piketty, to say in effect that if we as a society are unwilling or unable to compensate the losers, then the trade regime as now practiced is unjustified and should be changed. Their position could be summed up as: it is politically immoral to knowingly create losers and then fail to help them.

Perspective 2 is clearly an improvement over perspective 1, both as a descriptive theory and for its prescriptive claims as well. It indeed recognizes that globalization (meaning increased trade and reduced trade barriers) may be good in some respects but it is also bad in others. It harms *some* people; it is therefore not unequivocally good.[13]

In addition to this, thoughtful proponents of perspective 2, generally on the left of the political spectrum, also criticize specific trade deals, which are no longer blindly accepted, as in position 1. As Joseph Stiglitz and others have noted, many trade deals today cannot be justified along the lines advocated by Adam Smith and David Ricardo centuries ago. This is because the countries involved in, for instance, the proposed TPP, already have low trade barriers with one another. Whatever benefits are achieved through comparative advantage and specialization are currently being achieved. They require no new trade deal. This leads us to rightly ask the follow-up question: why do we need a TPP (or other similar deals)? What is its purpose, if reducing trade barriers is already an accomplishment?

The answer generally is to enact policies, from patent protections to reduced regulations, that will benefit large corporations. We already have free trade--new agreements being proposed are frequently about "non-tariff barriers to trade", which in practice means they are efforts to eliminate regulations and other laws that place any limits on the behavior of firms and their ability to increase profits. They are indeed, as Noam Chomsky aptly calls them, "investor rights agreements." They aim to enshrine non-trade related policies that will benefit the global rich, both as individuals and as corporations.[14]

These trade deals can be and are rightly rejected by many figures in both parties in the USA and are often unpopular with the broader public.

There is, however, a third perspective, which builds on some of these critiques and takes them in a further, more radical direction: The global trade regime as it has been practiced for the past few decades is actually bad for most people. This critique is not so much about winners and losers as it is about the fact that the global trade regime, as it has really existed, has by and large just produced losers.[15]

This may seem radical or naïve or both. Certainly the economics profession, Wall Street and the rest of the corporate world would reject this position, not to mention policy and party elites in DC, and the broader punditocracy. It is, at the same time, I think fairly obviously true, at least with regard to the wealthy countries of the world. Among major political figures, Bernie Sanders stands out for his opposition to key components of the global trade regime. As he noted in a January 2020 debate, "NAFTA, permanent normal trade relations (PNTR) with China, other trade agreements were written for one reason alone. And that is to increase the profits of large multinational corporations. And the end result of those two, just PNTR with China...and NAFTA, cost us some 4 million jobs, as part of the race to the bottom."[16] That fundamentally sums up the third perspective that I will advocate here.

Sanders is right. Let's look at the evidence. Consider the following points, often iterated but rarely appreciated in their full significance, comparing life now in the USA to life in the USA in the 1970s:

1) we work more hours on average while at the same time many working poor struggle with underemployment.[17]

2) we spend more time each week commuting to and from work.

3) we sleep less.

4) we spend more of our income on housing (be it rent or mortgage payments), which in turn has led to a cascading wave of evictions and foreclosures.[18]

5) more young people in their 20s and 30s live with their parents than any time since World War 2.

6) we spend much more money on education while high school and college graduation rates are stagnating.[19]

7) life expectancy is actually going down for substantial portions of the American population (an

absolutely catastrophic fact that has only previously happened in countries with a massive depression or civil war).[20]

8) we spend more on medical care than in the 1970s.

9) we spend more on childcare than in the 1970s.

10) we have less job security.

11) even though as a society we are more educated and work more hours than we did in the 1970s, most households are making about the same amount of money as they made in the 1970s (which, given that we work more hours and have to spend more of our income on education, housing, and healthcare, means that we are more poor. Not stagnating, but *worse* off). As David Blanchflower notes, real weekly pay in the United States today is below its 1972 level.[21]

11) a substantial portion of citizens have been downgraded from secure, well-compensated manufacturing jobs to low-paying, insecure service sector jobs, with the decline in income, benefits, status, and self-esteem that this entails.

12) our retirement benefits are smaller than in the 1970s (and are often non-existent).

13) we are currently suffering from a massive opioid epidemic that now claims upwards of 100,000 lives a year in the USA.[22]

14) for the first time in American history student debt is surpassing all other forms of debt and a generation of youth are entering the workforce with tens of thousands of dollars of debt, just as

they start their careers and hope to start a family. 15) through some combination of automation, trade, and domestic policy millions of well-compensated, secure, respected, unionized factory jobs have been lost.[23]

Sadly, one could go on.[24]

Can the existence of cheap consumer electronics (dvds, cds, iphones, etc) really justify those terrible consequences? Can it outweigh them to the point that we are better off suffering all those deprivations provided we can get cheap cellphones? Because that is basically the thought it takes to accept that the global trade regime has been good for those in wealthy countries.

This is not a straw man: it is the literal justification offered by the economics profession for increased global trade. Trade leads to the production of more goods, therefore it is good.
(With no attention to incomes, employment, job security, mental health, essential public goods like housing, education, and healthcare, nor to negative consequences such as increased drug abuse, suicide, mental illness, despair, and collapsing towns. Ordinary citizens, struggling to pay their bills and make ends meet, have to experience these negative effects. Prominent economics professors are generally immune. As I discuss more in chapters four and five, this disparity in lived experience matters. It is one of many

reasons to oppose elitism as a worldview and to oppose the elite rule that it justifies).

As an aside, some might claim that we are better off—violent crime is lower than it was decades ago (though starting to climb again), traffic deaths are down, medical advances help many people live longer and more physically comfortable lives. The problem is that these are beside the point. None of these positive gains in recent decades are the result of the global trade regime. We could have all of these benefits and also construct a global trade regime that wasn't devastating to the majority of ordinary citizens in America and Europe.

But, the critic might respond, couldn't a similar argument be made against my position? Just as the positive advances in recent decades in the US are not primarily due to the global trade regime, perhaps the negative consequences that I've outlined above are also not the consequence of the global trade regime? Might some distinct, US-specific, factors have caused the decline in living standards for so many Americans? Jonathan Rothwell, for instance, argues that the power of the professional classes to limit competition for their services is an important contributing factor to growing inequality in the US.[25] This is a significant and ultimately empirical question. And indeed, there are many factors, some attributable to American politics, that have contributed to the rampant growth of inequality and decline in living standards in the United States.

It is necessary to be clear here. The global trade regime of recent decades is only one contributing factor to the decline in living standards outlined above. It is not the only factor but it is an important one. Second, global trade does not have to be beneficial only to elites. This is a consequence of its current design combined with US-specific domestic policies that have hurt the working class. Some countries, particularly in Europe, have maintained stronger social programs, union protections, and other policies that have mitigated the damaging effects of the current global trade regime. For trade to be more fair it will require a global trade regime that is designed by and for the majority, not the elite, and for the US to adopt domestic policies that are more favorable to ordinary workers. As for the US, the biggest factor in addition to trade has been the enactment of anti-union laws at the state and federal level and the failure to enforce federal union protections in any meaningful way.[26] Collectively, these have dramatically lowered the bargaining power of American workers.

What does this look like in practice? First is the well-documented decline in union membership in the United States, from a postwar high of around one-third of the workforce to around 10 percent of all workers today. This is due to unfriendly labor laws at the state and federal level, unfriendly court decisions, and lax enforcement of labor rules and regulations by the federal government. (Indeed, federal worker protections may border on non-existent when Republicans control the executive branch.) In addition, corporations have mounted massive, well-funded and well-researched efforts to destroy unions and to crush new attempts at unionization. Why does this matter? Because as has been documented by social scientists, unionization contributes to income equality and better living conditions for working and middle class Americans. Unions raise wages and benefits for working class Americans. The decline of unions means the growth of inequality.[27]

But trade, as it has been practiced, has likely also destroyed many jobs. This isn't an absurd claim—indeed it is exactly what is supposed to happen when trade barriers are removed. Inefficient industries in the US will fail (and the jobs they provide will disappear), hopefully to be replaced by more productive industries and better jobs. Obviously it is the second part of this equation that has not panned out.[28] Elites, be they in government, the academy, Wall Street, big oil, the media, or Silicon Valley, generally don't see this or are deaf to these negative effects. This is at least partly because these elites have benefited from many of the same policies that have hurt ordinary Americans.

Note as well an important point that is often neglected. The idea of comparative advantage says that everybody will be better off if each country produces what it can produce most efficiently. *Better off* here means that global GDP will be at its highest, since this is the scenario in which the countries of the world produce the most goods. But this is an incomplete picture of welfare. First of all, there is nothing in the theories of Smith and Ricardo (nor any reason to think so today) that says that countries producing for their comparative advantage will create an adequate quantity of rewarding, well-compensated jobs. Indeed, in an era of technological advancement and automation it is possible that global trade will destroy far more jobs than it creates. As manufacturing in the United States either moved overseas (to countries where it could be done cheaper) or was automated (and thus cheaper, and more efficient, than employing many people), it may well have been replaced by a smaller number of good paying jobs in financial services, IT, and other areas in which America specializes. The remainder of jobs created in the wake of globalization may largely be low-wage, insecure, service sector jobs (precisely the types of jobs which can't be moved overseas).[29]

In other words, as the American economy shifted more towards its speciality of high-level global services, ideas, and products, it may have, in aggregate, lost many good jobs. This will strike the average citizen as obvious and the political, economic, and intellectual elite as heretical. But this, again, does not contradict the ideas of Smith and Ricardo with regard to trade. Indeed, a reduction of trade barriers has led to different countries specializing in various products, as expected. There is nothing about such specialization that guarantees good jobs, let alone many of them. It is perfectly possible, even plausible in an era of advancing automation, for global trade to lead to a higher global GDP and to a lower quantity of well-compensated jobs. This is because highly-productive industries may, especially in technologically advanced countries, only need a small number of workers to provide their products.[30]

Additionally, Smith and Ricardo say nothing with regard to the distribution of GDP. A global trade regime could lead to higher GDP in the US and lower living standards for the majority of citizens, if its benefits are concentrated at the top. Indeed, this appears to be precisely what has happened. Recent research has found that 53 million American workers earn $10.22 an hour, which adds up to about $18,000 per year in gross income. As the authors of this study note, "basic costs of living (housing, food, child care, transportation, health care, taxes) frequently outpace earnings from low-wage jobs, even in families with more than one worker." The global trade regime is not the only cause of this (they also cite automation, declining unionization, and concentrated market power, to name a few) but it is almost certainly a major factor.[31]

This low standard of living for so many Americans is connected to growing inequality, with benefits increasingly concentrated at the top. In *Who Stole the American Dream?* Hedrick Smith offers a truly startling figure: if the income distribution in America today was the same as a few decades ago, the bottom 80% of income earners would collectively receive an additional $750 billion per year in income. That income over recent decades has been shifted to the top 20% and specifically the top 1% (and .1%) of Americans, to the detriment of everyone else.[32]

Stated in different terms, in 1980 the bottom 50% (half of America!) used to earn about 20% of all income, whereas now they earn just 12% of income. Yes, you read that right, the bottom half of Americans earn 12% of all American income.[33] It cannot be overstated how profoundly unequal America has become and how devastating this has been for millions of citizens. Thomas Piketty, in his influential *Capital in the 21st Century*, went so far as to suggest that America is now creating an *experiment* in what happens when a society allows historically unprecedented income inequality. These developments are not incidental either. They are directly tied to a global trade regime, and a global economy more broadly, that is dominated by and serves the interests of economic and political elites. It is not run by or for ordinary Americans (or ordinary people anywhere in the world, for that matter).

At the end of the day, there is considerable empirical evidence that the global trade regime, combined with domestic policies that concentrate market power at the top and harm poor and middle income Americans, has destroyed many industries (famously manufacturing) that once provided good, middle-class jobs. Don't be fooled by the optimists who point to statistics regarding American manufacturing productivity or output. We are concerned with good jobs here and these have declined massively. Factories that used to employ thousands now employ hundreds, perhaps dozens.

There has indeed been something like a global race to the bottom, in which mobile global capital places pressure on governments around the world to weaken labor protections and reduce environmental regulations while also pressuring employers to lay off workers, cut wages and benefits, automate jobs, and relocate to locations with cheaper labor. As David Blanchflower notes, "globalization had weakened workers' bargaining power and the big decline in 2008 and 2009 made that obvious for all to see. In the recovery, even if employers had the ability to pay more, they had no need to. What was true then is true now. Workers care about job security, fear losing their jobs, and have little bargaining power. That is why wage growth isn't rocketing."[34]

To fully buy into claims made on behalf of the current global trade regime we have to believe that its massive benefits have been so outweighed by some other, unnamed factor, that living standards for the majority of Americans are declining in spite of the miraculous benefits of trade. What could this other factor be? Perhaps the global trade regime itself is a key factor in such devastation.

This does not mean that we should or could end trade, nor would we want to. What it means is that global institutions, trade treaties, domestic regulations, and laws need to be rewritten so that global trade benefits ordinary citizens in all countries, not a global corporate elite.

We also need to be more attentive to the socially destructive effects of rapid change, particularly when it is defined by job loss, deindustrialization, and the devastation of rural and small town communities. Consider a fitting passage from E.F. Schumacher, who, in his famous *Small is Beautiful*, provided a profound critique of conventional economic thinking:

"The life, work, and happiness of all societies depend on certain "psychological structures" which are infinitely precious and highly valuable. Social cohesion, cooperation, mutual respect, and above all, self-respect, courage in the face of adversity, and the ability to bear hardship—all this and much else disintegrates and disappears when these "psychological structures" are gravely damaged. A man is destroyed by the inner conviction of uselessness. No amount of economic growth can compensate for such losses—though this may be an idle reflection, since economic growth is normally inhibited by them."[35]

Political theorist Sheldon Wolin notes similarly that "a worker may have invested much of his adult life in a particular job and in a particular community." When constructing trade deals we should as a polity acknowledge that workers have a certain claim to maintain their way of life and the dignity and purpose that it brings. Unfortunately, in the past, governments negotiating trade deals as well as individual firms pursuing higher profits have acted on the principle that "in the interests of efficiency a firm is justified in closing down a plant and relocating it or eliminating it altogether."[36]

Economists and other defenders of the status quo could respond to this critique in many ways, from theories about how the world works to normative claims about how things ought to be to concrete empirical evidence.

One thing they might say: if everyone subscribed to this line of thinking, specifically that small, diffuse benefits in the form of economic growth or lower prices are outweighed by the concentrated pain of job loss and dislocation, then the economy could never advance. Technological gain, after all, creates winners and losers. There is truth to Joseph Schumpeter's claim that capitalist technological change is a process of "creative destruction." If we eliminate the destruction we also eliminate the progress.

This is a challenge but it is not very convincing. The above critic will likely say, as many economists do, that if government policy acted as I am suggesting, we never would have moved from an agrarian economy to an industrial and now post-industrial one, due to Luddite attitudes regarding economic change. But this analogy is inaccurate. Historically and today, agrarian workers *willingly* leave behind agrarian jobs for industrial jobs in urban centers because these new jobs, however dangerous, ill-compensated, and miserable, are better than the old agricultural jobs.

(Note, this is not a defense of sweatshops. These jobs are still terrible and should be made better through unionization, better pay and benefits, fewer hours, more safety, and a range of other pro-worker policies).

Trade policy is different. People with decent,

often very well-compensated jobs (good pay, benefits, vacation), jobs that also often have considerable respect and status, *unwillingly* lose their jobs and are often forced, through loss of income, to accept lower-paying, less secure, low-status jobs. That is, they are forced to lose a good job and take a bad job.

If industrialization had been like this of course it wouldn't have happened, at least without massive coercion, because people would not en masse leave behind good jobs for worse ones by choice. But this is arguably what many trade deals have done in recent decades.

Nor should we accept justifications of economic policy that claim reducing incomes in the developed world is the only way to raise incomes in underdeveloped countries. Do not accept claims from global elites that pit the poor and working classes of the rich countries against the poor and working classes of the poor countries. Domestic economic policies and global trade regimes can be designed in ways that benefit all working classes across a range of countries. In so far as some people's wealth must decline to benefit the poorest countries, it should be the oligarchs, the broader one percent, and the upper bounds of the professional classes who see higher taxes and limits on their wealth accumulation. These are the people who have benefited the most from the economic developments of the past few decades and it is time for them to pay their share back to the rest of us.

While economists tend to focus on the quantity of goods produced in a national economy (or region, city, etc.) they also need to focus on how those goods are acquired, i.e. through a well-paying, secure job. To ignore this is to ignore half the picture. Forms of global trade that undermine the latter are deeply problematic, even if they succeed in supplying the former.

More broadly, imagine if other policies were justified the way trade deals too often are: policy X will harm many middle and working class people but it will also help some and hopefully in aggregate it will do more good than bad. Citizens would rightly reject such policies.

These developments are deeply interwoven with the decline of political legitimacy in the long-standing democracies of the world. They are often qualitative in nature and hard to pin down with large-scale data. This is not to deny that empirical data is valuable, just to recognize its limits. Stagnant and declining incomes, benefits, and job security can be quantified. But as earlier generations of conservatives knew, the economy is not the entire story.[37]

Chris Hedges, in his recent book *America: The Farewell Tour* describes the non-economic aspects of

43

this decline: "A decline in status and power, an inability to advance, a lack of education and health care, and a loss of hope are crippling forms of humiliation. This humiliation fuels loneliness, frustration, anger, and feelings of worthlessness. In short, when you are marginalized and rejected by society, life often has little meaning. There arises a yearning among the disempowered to become as omnipotent as the gods."[38] This is arguably part of the reason why authoritarian populists are appealing to so many around the world today, particularly in the longstanding democracies of the world.

In a similar vein in the 1980s Sheldon Wolin recognized that growing "competition undercut[s] the settled identities of job, skill, and place and the traditional values of family and neighborhood which are normally the vital elements of the culture that sustains collective identity."[39] To put it more colloquially, as our many towns and neighborhoods have unraveled we have increasingly lost what Bruce Springsteen both celebrates and laments as "the ties that bind." This loss of identity and social ties in turn leads to a feeling of meaninglessness or incoherence on the part of negatively impacted individuals and communities: "incoherence means a lack of cultural and social place and a lack of support systems that enable individuals to resist or to cushion marginalization."[40]

This is precisely what is seen by ordinary Americans and missed by elites. It is not simply about lost income, though that is important, but is experienced as an all-out assault on community life. "When communities lose middle class manufacturing jobs," as Daniel Markovits points out, "not just earnings but also marriage and fertility rates fall, and mortality rates rise…families break apart. Children struggle in school. And adults strain simply to survive."[41] Only now, after many decades of devastation, are we starting to take account of this as a nation.

Higher education, which I discuss in chapter five, is a key part of the problem and helps us to understand the cluelessness so often displayed by elites on this topic. As Harry Boyte notes, "higher education bears a significant share of the responsibility, educating professionals to be mobile individualists who are detached from the communities in which they work and the cultures from which they come and who see people in terms of insufficiencies, as demanding customers or needy clients."[42] But most citizens, even in wealthy countries like the United States, are not global jetsetters. They are deeply embedded in local communities. When these communities suffer, they suffer with them, for ordinary citizens and the rich ties that bind us and give us meaning comprise the various communities in which we exist. When these unravel, the social and economic consequences are disastrous.

Similarly, political scientist Adam Przeworski recognizes that with declining incomes comes "an epochal change of expectations: perhaps for the first time in 200 years many people believe that their offspring will not lead better lives than they do...the erosion of the belief in intergenerational progress may well be historically unprecedented and its political consequences are ominous."[43] Again, it is hard to overstate how momentous this is. Stagnant incomes, rising living costs, declining life expectancy—every one of these factors runs against the core legitimizing principles of modern capitalist democracies. How are they to sustain themselves when the prospect of a better future no longer hovers on the horizon? How are we to understand a society not in a great depression that is nevertheless witnessing shrinking life spans? A simple way to put it is to recognize that such a society is not functioning well. When this happens it tends to delegitimize elite actors within the political system and the broader institutional features of that system, as we are seeing today in the United States and many other democracies around the world.

It is difficult to explain exactly how economic stagnation, inequality, and loss of status lead to authoritarian populism, though these features are often connected. Empirical evidence suggests that severe financial crashes do lead to increases in support for right-wing authoritarians, but in other situations the evidence is mixed. Sometimes stagnation leads to a rise in right-wing authoritarianism, sometimes it doesn't. This is probably because these factors are complex, amorphous, and hard to isolate into discrete, measurable variables. These economic problems are often not sufficient to cause a rise in authoritarian populism and sometimes not even necessary (some European countries that seem to be thriving have nevertheless seen a rise in authoritarians). But they are still clearly contributing factors. Qualitative research confirms this, as does journalism, as does common sense for all outside elite bubbles.

But it is hard to explain exactly how this operates. Economic stagnation makes people more open to authoritarian populism without guaranteeing that it will emerge. But they will be increasingly receptive to its siren song, particularly if media outlets and/or political figures start to appeal to such instincts.

As Pippa Norris and Ronald Inglehart report, risk of poverty, economic insecurity, and general economic hardship correlate with greater support for populism and less trust of authorities. This does not necessarily mean the populace becomes more supportive of authoritarians. After all, there are populists who are pro-democracy and anti-authoritarian. But it does complement my thesis that times of distress and institutional disfunction lead to the public being more receptive to a range of populist appeals (both left democratic populism and right authoritarian populism).[44]

It is not surprising that "reported levels of personal income insecurity may reflect a more general feeling of hard-times."[45] Other studies by political scientists have found similar results, namely "that insecurity—the share of individuals experiencing substantial resource declines without adequate financial buffers—has risen steadily since the mid-1980s for virtually all subgroups of Americans."[46] Furthermore, it should come as no surprise, given extreme levels of economic inequality, that such insecurity is more common, and more extreme, among the least educated and poorest. Recent surveys found that nearly half of Americans did not have enough money saved up to pay for an unexpected $400 emergency.[47]

Norris and Inglehart note that in 2016 "Trump performed best in places where the economy was at its worst, beating Clinton in counties with slower job growth and lower wages."[48] They also recognize other factors are at play, because these areas correlate with older, whiter, more conservative voters. Still, there is something to the economic thesis. It is *part* of the story. As the quantitative research indicates, economic struggles are strongly tied to distrust of conventional authorities and support for outsider populists.[49]

Psychologist Keith Payne documents similar findings as well. Economic hardship makes people more cruel towards outsiders and those perceived as different, by looking for scapegoats.

What is the upshot of this analysis? First, due to a variety of factors, living standards have declined across a range of metrics for many, perhaps an overwhelming majority, of Americans. Global trade, in addition to automation, declines in union membership, changing norms on executive pay, growing inequality, financial deregulation, and other pro-corporate public policies, has contributed to this decline.

Second, trade policy is too important to be left to economists. Trade policy, like all economic policies, is fundamentally a political question. That is, it can be informed by expert research but the discipline of economics cannot tell us what trade deals we should sign, which organizations we should join, and so on, because these involve questions of values. What do we value as a society? What do we want to promote? These questions don't have social scientific answers, regardless of what those at prominent think tanks and universities tell us. We cannot undo all the changes that globalized trade has wrought but we can change our political calculus for the future. When it comes to future trade deals, political and economic elites should listen more carefully to the broader citizenry, with their justified skepticism of trade deals. This will involve a different calculus. As I have suggested above, economists, and scholars more broadly, don't know how to effectively weigh the cost of job loss, dislocation, disrupted communities, and blighted neighborhoods. These are catastrophic costs. We must very carefully consider any policy that will inflict them before enacting it, if ever. The prospect of slightly cheaper consumer goods, particularly unnecessary electronics, is not worth this cost.[50]

Third, trade is not inherently bad. What needs to change is how it is practiced. The current global trade regime, and new future trade deals, must be organized around ecological sustainability and raising the living standards of the global working classes. This means, fundamentally, that future trade deals cannot be written by corporate lawyers in secret, as they now are.[51]

Again, this is the story of what happens when an important component of the economy, trade policy, is left in the hands of political, intellectual, and economic elites. Not only have they operated on flawed models of how the world works, they have enacted policies that have primarily benefited fellow elites and the broader professional classes, to the detriment of the majority of workers. A new set of policies that benefit workers of all colors and nationalities will be needed to undo these decades of damage.

CHAPTER THREE: INEQUALITY

Much like the negative consequences of American trade policy, decades of growing economic inequality are the inevitable product of a political system dominated by a cloistered set of elites and their elitist worldview.

The tension between democracy and elitism necessarily connects to conversations on inequality. In particular, the extreme forms of economic inequality that now define life in the United States. They are seen not just in massive disparities in income and wealth but also in status, dignity, life expectancy, physical and mental health, and political power. This chapter focuses on economic inequality, not because it necessarily determines all the other forms inequality can take but because it is easier to measure and to trace its influence into all domains and experiences of human life.

A simplistic form of Marxism treated the economy as a foundation that directly determined all other domains of life. In the 21st century we have a more sophisticated understanding of how messy and interconnected all aspects of human life are, without any one-way arrows directly determining everything. Nevertheless, while the economy may not determine all aspects of life, extreme economic inequality is a toxin, one that slowly but surely poisons all areas of human experience. It grants to some longer life, greater status, more resources, and more political power. It is as central to a discussion of democracy and elitism as any topic can be. These thoughts guide the discussion that follows.

Some thinkers, particularly among economists and libertarian philosophers, argue that economic inequality in itself does not matter, only absolute living standards. So, for instance, as long as the worst off attain a decent standard of living (however we define it), then a society is just, regardless of inequality. As the philosopher Harry Frankfurt says, "the widespread conviction that equality itself and as such has some basic value as an independently important moral ideal" is mistaken.[52]

I think this perspective is clearly wrong. Economic inequality is a problem in itself and one that directly relates to elite dominance of the American polity and economy. This does not mean that a perfectly equal distribution of wealth and income is possible, or necessarily even desirable. What it does mean is that there are strong reasons to be opposed to inequality, particularly in the extreme form it takes today in the United States and elsewhere. Economic inequality is not an on-off switch; rather, it operates on a spectrum. We can have more or less of it. As economic inequality increases, the negative consequences increase. As I discuss below, economic inequality *as such* and the consequences of economic inequality cannot be easily separated, contrary to Frankfurt's assertion.

Before moving on it will be helpful to very briefly summarize some facts on economic inequality. We can measure economic inequality in many ways, including differences in life expectancy, access to medical care, safety of neighborhoods, incarceration rates, food deserts, unemployment and regional job opportunities, disease and chronic health conditions, drug abuse, suicide, crime, and so on, but the easiest path is to consider income and wealth inequality. These broadly correlate with the above criteria, in that those with higher incomes and wealth tend to individually suffer from fewer of these problems and tend to live in areas that have fewer problems as well. This is also likely more than a mere correlation, in that there is good reason to believe that having access to more economic resources directly leads to a reduction in various negative social outcomes.

Okay, let's talk inequality. Depending on how you

measure it, the top one percent of Americans earn between 20-25% of all yearly income that is made in America. This is the highest concentration of income among the top one percent since the Great Depression. Such levels were only reached again on the eve of the Great Recession in 2007-2008 and have remained largely unchanged since then. The top ten percent of income earners take home upwards of fifty percent of all income in America. This number should sound shocking. Yes, 90% of Americans must fight over half of the pie, while ten percent comfortably enjoy the other half.[53]

The numbers on wealth inequality are even more extreme. By most measures, the top one percent of Americans own around 40% of all the wealth. The top ten percent has between 80-90% of the wealth. The bottom half of Americans effectively have no wealth, i.e. they own nothing of value and have no meaningful accumulated savings. Remarkably, these numbers may actually understate how severe inequality has become, given the ability of the wealthy to store considerable assets overseas and to disguise income in various ways.[54] It also doesn't include favorable bankruptcy and real estate laws or other tax breaks available only to the wealthy. Furthermore, the tax system is structured such that the richest Americans actually pay a lower percentage of their income in taxes than working and middle class Americans. This is largely because, as economists Emmanuel Saez and Gabriel Zucman observe, "capital income, in varying degrees, is becoming tax-free."[55]

Given the overwhelming evidence that economic inequality has risen dramatically since the 1970s, why should we care? There are five basic reasons why economic inequality is objectionable. In brief form they are as follows:

1)   The empirical objection: Societies that are deeply unequal generally do not provide a high quality of living for their poorest members. This is not surprising, for societies that allow gross inequality tend to not be very concerned with the poor. Even as European countries grew wealthier with the industrial revolution, living standards for the poor and working class remained abysmally low until these countries became more equal in the twentieth century. It should come as no surprise, empirically, that the societies in which the worst off have had good standards of living have also tended to be relatively equal, like those seen in Scandinavia. Furthermore, there is reason to believe that extreme inequality reduces economic mobility, i.e. people have a harder time improving their lot in deeply unequal societies. As David Blanchflower notes, "there is clear evidence that as inequality rises, mobility declines. Countries with the highest mobility had the lowest inequality."

Thus, class inequality increasingly sediments into a form of rigid caste inequality when societies are deeply unequal.[56]

2)   The conceptual objection: This relates to the point made above. In a world with finite resources, even the wealthiest societies have limits on how many goods and services they can produce. Therefore, to improve the lives of the worst off inevitably requires reducing inequality by taxing and limiting the wealth acquisition and incomes of the best off. In other words, helping the worst off requires reducing inequality.

3)   The moral objection: It is wrong for a small number of individuals to monopolize such a large share of society's resources. More specifically, it is wrong to construct a society in which the majority must work long hours and spend their entire paychecks on life's necessities while a subset of oligarchs (whose societal contributions are of questionable value) live in leisure and don't struggle over acquiring resources. How could we justify a society like this, where some live in impossible luxury and the rest struggle to get by? Deeply unequal societies impose lives of tremendous hardship on many and unearned comfort for a few. This in turn leads to deeply unequal status, in which many suffer from a lack of recognition while a small minority benefits from the added psychological com-

fort and self-esteem that go with high status lives. In addition, the majority of overworked, under-compensated workers will struggle to fully develop their human potentialities. Humans are complex, creative creatures with considerable analytic and emotional ranges of experience—they cannot adequately enjoy or develop these without the time and energy to do so. Currently, a majority of workers lack such time and energy. John Rawls as well as many other moral and political philosophers would call such a society unjust. I agree and think this point is distinct from but importantly related to the following one.[57]

4)   The political objection: Distinct from the previous one (but related), it is politically wrong to have high levels of economic inequality because they inevitably lead to unequal political power and corrupt the political process. Throughout human history economic power and wealth have translated to political power. This is not a mere correlation. We know why it happens. Those with economic power are able to effectively influence (or take over) the political system, through both subtle and overt means. Economic inequality undermines political equality and thus democracy. It is unjust from a democratic perspective.

5) The psychological objection: This is increasingly demonstrated through recent psycho-

logical research by scholars like Keith Payne. Humans are hardwired through evolution to care about inequalities in power, wealth, and status. Even if things stay the same for us, we perceive injustice when others get ahead. More broadly, we are constantly comparing ourselves to others, both consciously and subconsciously. When we see ourselves being left behind it hurts. We suffer increased stress, anxiety, depression, and rage, and are more likely to become addicted to drugs and/or attempt suicide. The destructive effects of inequality are felt deeply inside of each of us and to be lower on a long, unequal social ladder is to live a shorter, less pleasant life. The research on this is overwhelming. Inequality creates a vicious circle for those at the bottom, with less happiness, more stress, fewer resources and opportunities, and ultimately shorter lives. The absolute standard doesn't matter—in a really unequal society those at the top push down on those at the bottom.

As Payne notes, "our relentless social comparing means that our own net worth is never truly separate from that of the haves and have-nots around us. When the rich get richer, everyone else feels poorer."[58] In a highly competitive society, in which a small number of winners receive most of the economic rewards, there are many losers. As noted above, this leads to increased anxiety, fear of unemployment, and lower work satisfaction. Workers in such situations will also be too scared to press for raises. As Payne notes, "the extreme inequality seen today in CEO pay is likely to undermine job satisfaction, team performance, and product quality. It may inspire workers to slack off, steal, and sabotage."[59]

Jonathan Rothwell, in *A Republic of Equals*, reiterates the related empirical objection (objection 1), namely that deeply unequal societies don't provide an adequate standard of living for their poor. In the unequal United States, "the basic point is simple: economic growth is less effective at raising the living standards of the masses —and a small slice of elites reaps a huge chunk of the gains. This is likely to strike many people as unfair."[60]

The solution, too, is simple, as Payne states: "In practical terms, reducing inequality means both raising the bottom rungs of the social ladder and lowering the top ones."[61] This directly relates to points 1 and 2. Raising those at the bottom requires, to some extent, placing limits on how high those at the top can climb. There is no empirical evidence that we benefit from private individuals controlling wealth of $1 billion or more and considerable evidence that it does serious harm. Nor are there good moral or other theoretical reasons for concentrating so much wealth into so few private hands.

Rousseau in his *Discourse on Inequality* laments a world in which "a handful of men be glutted with superficialities while the starving multitude lacks necessities." To those who would object that in a rich country like the US the poor no longer lack necessities, consider the following: tens of thousands die every year due to a lack of health coverage, thousands go into medical bankruptcy, thousands die from forgoing insulin shots and other needed treatments, the homeless freeze to death in the winter, and the poor overall live shorter, less healthy lives (and often don't have access to healthy food, because of limited money and/or food deserts). The poor in an unequal society do in fact experience such injustices as life or death matters. They do die.

The point here is not simply that these people do not have enough, though of course they do not. It is that to remedy this would require public investments funded by increased taxes on the wealth and incomes of the richest Americans, as well as wage increases for ordinary workers that come out of the pockets of the executives and wealthy shareholders of these companies. To remedy the lack felt by those in the bottom half requires reducing the resources monopolized by those in the top half, particularly the absurdly concentrated incomes and wealth of the top one percent. It cannot be stressed enough that the lack of opportunity, dignity, resources, and political power experienced by those at the bottom is empirically and conceptually connected to the surplus of these same things possessed by those at the top.

It is no surprise that economic elites deny this point, choosing instead to focus on absolute standards in an effort to sever the connection between those at the bottom and those at the top. To recognize the above point leads us to demand that economic elites lose some (or all) of their economic power and its corollary, political power. This they are loathe to do, as is generally true of elites everywhere.

Political scientist Adam Przeworski, in his recent *Why Bother With Elections?*, offers several thoughts on how economic inequality leads to political equality. He concludes bluntly: "effective political equality is not possible in a socially and economically unequal society."[62] To continue, Przeworski describes how these negative feedback loops operate: "economic inequality results in political inequality; political inequality tilts government policies in favor of people with higher incomes. Hence, economic inequality perpetuates itself."[63] A deeply unequal society is an elite-dominated one, by definition. It is, at most, a partial democracy. To achieve more democracy in America requires a reduction in elite rule, which in turn requires a dramatic reduction in economic inequality.

There are other social costs resulting from economic inequality, borne largely by those at the bottom of the ladder. Relating to points 3 and 5, there is considerable evidence that wage increases lead to reductions in crime, as do drops in unemployment. This is partly a moral claim: those with low wages and those without work suffer unfairly as they try to pay bills and are more likely to turn to crime to make ends meet. We then turn around and punish them. This is wrong. The second part is the psychological component: to be without a decent paying job lowers morale, hurts self-esteem, and increases the likelihood of drug abuse, suicide, and crime. These are precisely the things that will define life for those on the bottom in a deeply unequal society.

Frankly, it is not clear if there are any compelling defenses of economic inequality and certainly not of the kind that now characterizes the economy of the United States. While those on the right may be tempted to dismiss such concerns, authors like Harry Frankfurt attempt to recognize some of these arguments against inequality while still claiming that inequality *per se* is not the problem. For instance, Frankfurt recognizes that economic inequality may be undesirable because it will "lead invariably to undesirable discrepancies of other kinds—for example, in social status, in political influence, or in the abilities of people to make effective use of their various opportunities and entitlements."[64]

But to grant this is to concede the entire argument. If, indeed, economic inequality leads to unequal, concentrated political power (my objection # 4), humiliating inequalities in status and respect (a version of my objection # 5), and the inability of the working masses to truly enjoy their freedom and develop themselves fully (objection # 3), these are damning reasons to oppose it. If these are not merely correlated, but in fact economic inequality is the, or one of the, main causes of such negative outcomes, then it must be opposed. It borders on incoherence to say, as Frankfurt does, that the direct consequences of inequality are bad but inequality itself is not bad. They are inseparable. They are one and the same, in the same way that drunk driving is bad. It makes no sense to say that drunk driving isn't the problem, only its negative consequences are.

Frankfurt also attempts to deny points 1 and 2, claiming that the "association of low social position and dreadful quality of life is not a matter of how things must necessarily be."[65] But as we have seen, a low social position and a low quality of life are inherently related. It is not so easy to pry apart absolute quality of life from relative quality. Indeed, it is not clear that there is any absolute standard for a good quality of life. As societies become wealthier in the aggregate the standard for a good life understandably and necessarily rises.

This is why deeply unequal societies will always fail to provide a sufficient quality of life for the worst off. They make available a richness and quality of life to a subset of citizens while depriving the remainder of such a decent life.

This is why comparisons between human living standards over the course of many centuries miss the point. The question is not whether people live longer now than in the year 1500 (they do) or whether this is good (it is), the question is whether political and economic systems distribute power, status, and resources in justifiable, fair ways. Those that are deeply unequal by definition do not, even if they provide some minimal resources to those at the bottom.[66] Furthermore, as a considerable amount of psychological research confirms, societies with considerable inequality have worse health outcomes and generally more crime, even when living standards in an absolute sense are high. They are also subjectively less pleasant. As Daniel Markovits wisely recognizes, "it feels better to be at the center of your own poorer society than on the margins of someone else's richer one." Yet this status and income exclusion, in which a majority of Americans arguably live "on the margins", is exactly what America looks like today. It is no more acceptable when dressed in a meritocratic guise.[67]

Thus, even "meritocratic" forms of inequality should be resisted. Discussing the distinction between democracy and "meritocratic" inequality, Sheldon Wolin expresses "the conviction that the democratic way of life is the best for the vast majority of human beings and that a meritocracy with a human face and the existence of a few tokens representing the remarkable diversity of American society are not synonymous with democracy but a parody of equalitarianism."[68] Unfortunately, "democracy has acquired a paradoxical status in American public rhetoric: it is universally praised while dismissed in practice as irrelevant or embarrassing to a meritocratic society."[69]

For the above reasons, inequalities in wealth, income, status, and power are to be opposed, even if elites claim their privileges on meritocratic grounds. In this sense too there are no final, absolute standards of living. When living standards increase this is undoubtedly a positive. But there is a corollary. As societies become wealthier, the living standard that all citizens have a right to claim inevitably rises. In any given society, when wealth and income are concentrated at the top, the decent quality of life attainable for everyone in that society will be denied to many of its citizens. This is exactly what happens in the United States today. The high quality of life possible today for every American is nevertheless denied to far too many because of concentrated wealth and power. The five objections to inequality outlined at the beginning of the chapter all fit contemporary

America. Concerns about living standards are inevitably relative. This is why inequality matters.

Centuries ago Rousseau longed for a society in which, as he put it, the poor could not be bought and the rich could not buy them. This would only be possible, of course, if economic resources were relatively equal in distribution. This would prevent the rich from having the power, status, and influence to "buy" the poor and dominate the political process. A basic measure of economic equality, in other words, is necessary for democracy to function. The meritocratic ethos embraced by elites today is antidemocratic in so far as it accepts "as legitimate vast differentials in income, education, power, culture, and health as long as these seem to be justified by the merit principles recognized by our society."[70] As noted above, such inequalities will infect, and over time, come to define the political process. It is high time we reduced them.

Reducing such inequalities will, in addition to improving the lives of the vast majority, decrease the unjust power and influence of economic and political elites. It will strengthen genuine democracy —rule by the people—at the expense of elite dominance. Need we say more?

CHAPTER FOUR: EXPERIENTIAL KNOWLEDGE

In the wake of 2016, which saw the passage of Brexit and the triumph of Donald Trump, it became increasingly common to hear various intellectual criticisms of democracy as it is currently practiced. Those on the left, particularly those sympathetic to populists like Bernie Sanders, should be aware of these arguments so that we are equipped to fend them off as they resurface. Perhaps serendipitously, two influential books were published in 2016 that both critique democracy from an elite perspective.

The first, Jason Brennan's *Against Democracy,* offered a host of philosophical arguments and empirical evidence regarding the failures of democratic politics and several reasons why we should consider switching to epistocracy, or rule by the most knowledgeable.[71]

Here I want to focus on the other book, *Democracy*

for Realists, coauthored by eminent political scientists Christopher Achen and Larry Bartels. This book, which was heralded by scholars and journalists alike, is not necessarily considered a work of elitism. The authors certainly don't suggest that we disenfranchise the less educated. Nevertheless, the text relies on and advances a number of key elitist arguments that are likely to be rehashed over and over in the coming years. They are worth delving into in more critical detail. To do so requires that we discuss not just democracy and elitism, but *knowledge*.

In the second part of this chapter I discuss the experiential knowledge that citizens acquire as workers and how this provides insights into the national economy that economists themselves often lack. This is an example of experiential knowledge that surpasses the professional knowledge of experts in its wisdom, groundedness, and insight.

Finally, in the third part I shift to a discussion of means tested and universal social programs, arguing that the experiences of ordinary citizens demonstrate that universal programs are more likely to be popular and enduring than supposedly "pragmatic" means tested programs. As with each chapter, the evidence and arguments tie into the broader thesis that elitism as a worldview is deeply misguided and elite rule is devastating for our democracy.

Achen and Bartels on political knowledge

What is knowledge? What do we mean when we say that we know something? Philosophers have spent centuries discussing these questions but I want to avoid the intricate debates that constitute the world of epistemology. Rather, in this section I am focused on *political* forms of knowledge and what I call *experiential* knowledge.

I begin this chapter by engaging with Christopher Achen and Larry Bartels' *Democracy for Realists* because it is the most influential recent attempt to tackle these questions from a more or less elitist perspective. Achen and Bartels devote hundreds of pages to the task of demonstrating that the American citizenry (and presumably the same goes for other countries) are profoundly ignorant on political matters and tend to engage in political activity largely on the basis of partisan and other group identities. Achen and Bartels are thus concerned with the same questions I am: Is there such a thing as specialized political knowledge? How much do ordinary citizens know? What can we expect of them as democratic participants? Achen and Bartels believe that this profound ignorance on the part of the citizenry requires a revision of how we theorize democracy and how we understand its practical reality.[72]

Elitists like Achen and Bartels also tend to present themselves as going against the grain of predominant social thought when in reality they are actually a part of the oldest tradition of the west. Since Plato, intellectual elites and the wealthy classes have offered many version of such arguments. In more recent years we see these arguments in philosophy, business schools, and across the social sciences. The vast wealth of research cited by Achen, Bartels, Jason Brennan, Bryan Caplan, and other elitists is evidence of this.

The elitist conceit is as follows: the citizenry is largely ignorant of policy specifics and cannot form correct political judgments. This in turn leads to bad policy being enacted in a democracy. Achen and Bartels, for instance, explicitly make this claim. There are many problems with it, some of which I discuss elsewhere. At its most basic, the problem with this perspective is that what citizens want does not tend to get enacted into policy because citizens have relatively little power in most representative democracies. Rather, economic elites tend to dominate this process. Contrary to the claims of Achen and Bartels, there is good reason to be *more deferential* to the citizenry. They possess a richer experiential knowledge than that found among political and economic elites, leading in part to different opinions on politics and economics. In keeping with the evidence and arguments of the preceding chapters, American democracy would actually benefit from less elite dominance and more popular rule, i.e. more genuine democracy. I elaborate on these points below.

Achen and Bartels, as with other elite-leaning accounts, don't consider experiential knowledge, although some of their interlocuters who want to defend democracy do gesture at it. An example of what experiential knowledge would look like in practice is seen in Albert Dzur's recent book *Democracy Inside,* in which he discusses experiments that allow students to participate in making key decisions in their schools. Other examples include efforts to get prisoners involved in education policy and other elements of the criminal justice experience. Dzur quotes a city manager who wisely notes that ordinary citizens are "not going to question [the policy specifics of] how we deliver the services as much as whether it is an appropriate service to be delivered and how it should be paid for. And those are issues I'm not sure there is a professional answer to."[73] Bravo! This city manager offers a perspective that is the perfect antidote to that offered by Achen, Bartels, and others with elitist convictions.

In addition, there are the potential broader benefits of direct citizen participation. The head of the Participatory Budgeting Project, Josh Lerner, describes some of the benefits of such direct participation among diverse citizens: "there is a deeper, qualitative impact of face-to-face engagement: transformative learning. By engaging in months of focused discussions and field research with diverse residents from all walks of life, participants often transform their views of both the community and themselves."[74]

Achen and Bartels, however, are operating with a very different view of the political world. For instance, they want to assess and rank the best presidents of the 20th century. In doing so they cite various historians as well as other academic studies that try to estimate, on a numeric scale, the quality of presidents over the 20th century. This fails to understand the nature of the political sphere. Assessing a good president may require knowledge and thoughtfulness but it is not akin to the professional judgment of a climate scientist, a chemist, an engineer, and so on. Political (and moral) judgments are not built on professional expertise: they are built around assessing what one values and how to achieve it politically. This doesn't mean all political judgments are equal but it does mean that experts cannot supply them—they are interdependent and developed through dialogue and action among citizens, and it is in the public sphere that we assess their value. This is what democracy is all about: citizens coming together to talk, work, and make decisions in concert when things aren't obvious, certain, scientifically given, mathematically clear, or philosophically settled. In light of this it is almost comical to attempt to assign numbers to individual presidents as objective rankings of their quality. The very central political question, "on what grounds are we assessing them?" is settled out of sight, beforehand, though it is the one question that matters in this case.

It should not be surprising that intellectual elites would draw on such assumptions, however. As Noam Chomsky noted half a century ago, "intellectuals, in interpreting history or formulating policy, will tend to adopt an elitist position, condemning popular movements and mass participation in decision-making, and emphasizing rather the necessity for supervision by those who possess the knowledge and understanding that is required (so they claim) to manage society and control social change."[75]

Contrary to the elitist perspective, what democracy requires is not technical expertise but a citizen ethos of "active care" in which citizens are concerned with and directed involved in maintaining democratic practices and a democratic way of life. Sheldon Wolin, one of democracy's wisest observers, helpfully explains: the democratic ethos "implies active care of things close at hand...[this] is not, however, a synonym for expert knowledge. Expert knowledge is typically predicated upon attitudes of detachment, upon disavowing personal involvement and disregarding historical associations."[76] But detachment from the personal stakes and places that compose the political sphere are precisely the traits that active, caring democratic citizens should not embrace.

When it comes to knowledge, for instance, Achen and Bartels want to suggest that the fundamental identities citizens possess, rather than their policy preferences, will drive their political decisions. So, as an example, they claim that one is pro-life because they are a Republican, and not Republican because they are pro-life. Their identity dictates their specific policy commitments. They provide plenty of evidence for this point, although much of it is unconvincing. There is no doubt that identity is central to politics. We can recognize this point without buying the entirety of Achen and Bartels' account. More on that in a moment. But first we need to get a better grip on the flawed elitist assumptions underlying their arguments.

For instance, there are plausible grounds for suggesting that the elite conclusions social scientists frequently draw from polling results are deeply flawed. Take the fact that polling answers to questions on war and peace vary dramatically depending on which terms are used. If you ask the public whether they support a military action, answers will differ depending on which of the following terms you use: "military force", "go to war", "aggression" and so on. Elitists think this means people are ignorant and lack settled, clear preferences, thus changing their answers based on subtle changes in poll wording. But this is not a sign of ignorance, it is a sign of understanding! Words have meaning. Those different phrases regarding war have different connotations and even imply different policies. Partly, they are loaded, so that some have positive connotations and others negative, which people rightly pick up on. (Some questions in effect are like asking, "do you support bad wars?" which people rightly answer "no" to.) Other questions actually imply completely distinct policies. "Use force" implies something light and quick, perhaps limited airstrikes. "Go to war" implies a costly, long-term commitment that could involve ground troops, heavy casualties, lots of money, endless occupation, and so on. These are different things! It is reasonable for citizens to have different answers to the questions "do you support the use of force?" and "do you support going to war?"

It is therefore not implausible to suggest that ordinary citizens are actually better at understanding poll questions than many social scientists. The social scientists say, in effect, citizens give different answers to these questions regarding war because they are ignorant, subject to subtle manipulation, and don't have fixed policy preferences. Ordinary citizens responding to polls, however, pick up on the fact that different wording implies different policies. They are right to have different answers because they are in fact being asked different questions!

This leads us to the following question: Why are elitists like Achen and Bartels (and many others) so intent on denying the obvious: that ordinary citizens are trying to work, have families, enjoy life, and make sense of a complicated world while also pursuing and following politics as best they can, and are generally doing a decent job of it? Why are these authors (and others like them) so focused on deflecting attention away from powerful elites? [77]

For them, "the problem is not so much that voters are necessarily irrational, but that most voters have very little real information, even about crucially important aspects of national political life." [78] The authors present themselves as engaging in an act of disillusionment—they are puncturing the bubble of American mythology regarding democracy, i.e. the common belief that informed citizens elect a government that then enacts the desires of the citizenry. By showing that citizens are often not well-informed, they hope to show that the celebratory image of democracy found in our schoolbooks and national holidays is false. But they, along with similar elitist accounts from other authors, never fully puncture the bubble. To fully puncture the bubble we must direct our gaze at the political and economic elites that disproportionately dominate our political system and who actually influence and make policy. To do so is to recognize that citizen ignorance is in many respects irrelevant, for elected governments do not enact what citizens want. They enact what the wealthy and organized business interests want.

In spite of all this, Achen and Bartels say on page 86 that politics in America would work better if the poor were more organized and involved. So it seems they want a kind of robust, mixed republicanism. They oppose pure democracy but don't want to remove the people entirely. In a strange reversal in tone and substance, after 300 plus pages of focusing on the ignorance and follies of the citizenry, the authors turn their attention toward elites, recognizing that "the most powerful players in the policy game are the most educated, the wealthy, and the well-connected." They rightly recognize that greater democracy requires "a greater degree of social and economic equality."[79] If, as Achen and Bartels suggest, a naive folk theory of democracy helps to prop up an elite-dominated status quo, what is the alternative? The answer seems obvious, and cuts against the grain of the majority of their work: to give more power to the people and to disempower the elites. But this is precisely what they spend most of the book arguing *against,* suggesting that it would be naive to seek to resolve democracy's problems with greater democracy.

Achen and Bartels, in *Democracy for Realists*, therefore represent an elitist position that is less hostile to democracy than Plato, as discussed in the introduction. They are willing to defend a mixed system of government such as the United States has while also criticizing claims for dramatically increasing citizen participation and direct democracy in the US. If they recognize that there is value in letting citizens participate in elections, why are they so hostile to progressive efforts to expand citizen participation? There are a number of reasons.

To begin with, they believe that citizens are not only factually ignorant but causally irrational. That is, citizens often fail to identify what governments are (or are not) responsible for and thus cannot effectively hold them accountable. For instance, in what they present as a powerful and damning indictment of the rationality of voters, Achen and Bartels demonstrate in chapter five of their book the impact that shark attacks and bad weather have had on elections. In general, when bad things happen, even things outside of the control of government (like weather or shark attacks), voters punish the incumbent party. In their words, "when voters endure natural disasters they generally vote against the party in power, even if the government could not possibly have prevented the problem."[80] To more accurately characterize their finding, when voters endure natural disasters, a small but potentially impactful number of them switch to voting against the incumbent party, at least partly because they attribute blame for the natural disasters to the incumbent in power. Rather than challenge the empirical findings, as some have done, I want to make a different point. So what?

Yes, that's right. So what? Does it matter if some voters base their political decisions on negative reactions to natural disasters? Elected politicians, even good ones, have no divine right to the throne. They are not being wronged by being voted out of office. Achen and Bartels might respond by saying that voters are harming themselves by thinking so irrationally. But it is not clear if this is true. It *is* clear that political elites harm voters when they rush into costly wars that kills thousands, displace millions, and generate regional and global instability. It *is* clear that economic elites harm voters when they engage in practices that generate financial instability and produce recessions that throw millions out of work, depress wages, foreclose homes, stunt growth, and concentrate wealth in a small number of hands.

Given decades of elite incompetence and malpractice, it is unconvincing to argue that they are more knowledgable, rational, or moral than the broader public. The elitist worldview, that ordinary citizens are ignorant of key political facts, irrational in their political reasoning, and objectively wrong in their political beliefs, doesn't hold up well under scrutiny. At the very least, elites impale themselves on the same charges that they thrust towards the broader citizenry.

Once again, as with all elitist accounts, we are left with the actual damning point, a question: Why are they so intent on absolving the powerful of responsibility for their wrongs by transferring it onto the populace? Is it because elitist thinkers tend to be powerful themselves? Influential elitists are not adjunct professors struggling to pay rent. They are not professors teaching ten classes a year at the teaching colleges that are the workhorse of American higher education and social mobility. They are, rather, highly-compensated professors at elite schools with income, status, security, and influence that make them borderline one-percenters. They can publish op-eds in major newspapers anytime they want, publish books when and on what topics they want with major publishers, command hefty speaking fees, and get public adulation for their research from academic and non-academic audiences alike. They are not average citizens. Maybe engaging in extended elitist argumentation is a not-so-subtle way of defending their own class.

This is not conspiratorial. The powerful want to defend their positions and they want to believe that they are making the world a better place, as we all do. To redirect blame away from political, economic, and intellectual elites and toward the broader populace is to do just that.

Perhaps in a different world, where elites were held to account for their malfeasance, we might point a secondary set of accusations against the public for failing to adequately hold misbehaving elites to account. But we live in no such world. The elitist perspective is a choice to redirect criticism away from the misbehavior of those in power to the broader public and the limited power that they possess. While working on this chapter *Jacobin* published a piece by Amber A'Lee Frost on the WeWork scandal. This scandal is not especially surprising, just the latest example of elite malfeasance and unjustified, euphoric group-think.[81] It is, in fact, all too mundane.

As I discussed in *Does Democracy Have a Future*, elitists are making a category mistake in their approach to politics. It is true that professional knowledge and expertise can exist in social science (someone is an expert on courts, or voting behavior, party formation, international law, etc.). This does not make them an expert on the political (the realm of human behavior concerning the general good and where forms of politics are practiced). That is because there is no such thing as expertise on the political. As Wolin aptly characterizes it, the political sphere is the realm in which "a free society composed of diversities can nonetheless enjoy moments of commonality when, through public deliberations, collective power is used to promote or protect the well-being of the collectivity."[82] The political is not a realm of science or philosophy. It is not a world of academic knowledge or expertise, but rather the sphere in which we decide how we want to organize ourselves collectively.

The *political* concerns us coming together and working in common, despite our differences, to make fundamental choices about the kind of society we want to live in, what laws we want, how we want our economy to function, and so on. We set up these standards intersubjectively through talk and action, including power struggles. It isn't always pretty. But fundamentally, debate and concerted effort help to establish the values that will guide a polity and they can change over time. The political world is, to put it differently, a world of public talk and public action.

As Samuel Stein explains, the political world is built around decisions in which "certain futures will be promoted while others are foreclosed. The rich and the poor will not share equally, and racial and gender divisions will be either dismantled or maintained. Things will get built or they won't, and they will go somewhere or other. These are all political decisions," not matters to be decided by experts. Indeed, it is incoherent to claim that there is a single, correct answer known by experts to questions such as "what should our cities look like?" Or "which citizens should benefit the most from macroeconomic policies?"[83]

Nevertheless, Achen and Bartels seek to criticize and dismiss "the unrealistic notion that ordinary citizens vote on the basis of detailed preferences regarding every issue that might conceivably come before their future leaders."[84] To call this a straw man argument would be generous. No democratic theorist has ever asserted such a notion, nor is it clear that the general, vague, "folk theory of democracy" that Achen and Bartels criticize has any proponents who would make such a preposterous claim. Furthermore, does any citizen on earth meet this standard, even among the most educated and politically informed? Of course voters don't have detailed awareness of "*every issue* that might conceivably come before future leaders." This is not possible nor is it necessary for democratic politics.

On another level it is downright strange how much effort elitists devote to showing the apparent ignorance and irrationality of the people. Achen and Bartels are at desperate pains, as are their many sources, to show that citizen political behavior is not what it appears to be. Liberal states electing and reelecting democrats and also voting for liberal referenda are apparently not evidence of citizens generally pursuing their political goals. Same for conservative states and citizens. Rather, it is all reductive—some outside source, identity, or influence is supposedly the cause of this behavior and in such a manner that the citizens don't get credit for knowledge or (much) instrumental rationality. Obviously we are all influenced by various sources—this is in part a good thing, for it is how we learn and grow —but in the end we have to treat people as at least somewhat aware of and responsible for their political beliefs and behavior. If one spent a lifetime researching Achen and Bartels we could probably claim to reduce their political beliefs to various external sources. While this might shed light on their backgrounds and influences, would it be convincing? Couldn't we better respect them, and reality, by recognizing that they, like other citizens, are basically aware of what they are doing and thinking?

Consider an analogy: elitists want citizens to answer lots of basic factual political questions. When they fail, elitists despair over the state of the electorate. But this is like asking someone for detailed driving directions, with every road name and every turn and distance. Just because they don't know those specific things doesn't mean they don't know how to get there. I can know where I'm going without remembering the names of all of the streets, the distance between them, the cardinal direction I am heading, the town I am in, and so on. Indeed, the political knowledge, wisdom, and gut instincts of the citizenry might resemble this more than the book learning desired by elitists.

In a sense this entire elitist exercise of Achen and Bartels is a mere preface to their real interest, which is to stress the importance of identity in politics. In so far as they claim that "social identities are diverse, complex, and profoundly interwoven with other politically relevant attitudes and opinions" there is no need to reject their perspective.[85] Individual and group identities *do* have a powerful influence on how we think and act in the political realm. But to argue that all political ideology and policy preferences are reducible to group identities, as they at times suggest, is to take this point too far. Furthermore, we can embrace many of their insights regarding the importance of group identity for politics without embracing the generally elitist thrust of their work. Identity and ideology are so interconnected that we can hardly differentiate them, let alone demonstrate how one influences or "causes" the other.

For instance, they argue that "when political candidates court the support of groups, they are judged in part on whether they can 'speak our language'...knowing those concerns, using that vocabulary, and making commitments to take them seriously is likely to be crucial for a politician to win their support."[86] This is undoubtedly true. But again, symbolic appeals to identity, to being "one of us" are hard to differentiate from particular policy goals and broad ideological commitments. Nor can these factors simply be disentangled and isolated in quantitative research—they interact with and impact one another. My identity feeds into and informs my specific political beliefs just as they feed into and inform my identity. Neither is prior. At times Achens and Bartels drift towards the tautological claim that any and all political behaviors are the product of more foundational identities, even when they appear to be driven by specific policy goals or explicitly held ideologies.[87]

At the end of the day the specific details of this debate may not matter that much. Ordinary citizens are neither as ignorant nor as irrational as these authors (and many others suggest). But they are of course influenced by how they understand themselves. Citizens and scholars alike would do well to recognize that group identities play a key role in the political realm. Citizens participate in politics on the basis of a complex mixture of both unconscious and conscious forms of identity, broad ideological commitments, specific policy goals, self-interest, vague concerns for justice, feelings of altruism, an attempt at understanding the common good, various related and unrelated beliefs, gut intuitions, emotions, and more. None of these factors determines the others in a direct line. To use older terminology, there is no base and super-structure here.

Elitists are correct that ordinary citizens do not participate in politics by engaging in an abstract, fully informed and philosophically reasoned thought process that leads them to pursue some enlightened, "correct" set of policies. Neither do elites, for that matter. But this was never a plausible account of human psychology or political action.[88] Nor is it necessary for one to embrace such an account to remain committed to a populist vision of participatory democracy. Contra elitism, participatory democracy can survive a healthy dose of realism.[89]

As political scientist Katherine Cramer observes about Wisconsin voters, "I heard people making sense of health care, education, and property taxes as a function of the kinds of people they believed themselves to be."[90] There is nothing irrational in such behavior and it likely is a central part of a feedback loop in which identity informs ideology and policy preferences which then feed back into and revise identity. Political belief, ideology, and identity are thus an ongoing process, not fixed points. To reiterate, none of this necessarily leads to elitism.

Experiential Knowledge and Economics

Having spent considerable time critiquing an elitist account of political knowledge it will now be helpful to spell out in more detail what the experiential knowledge of ordinary citizens might resemble in the real world.

What might experiential knowledge look like in practice? Take company layoffs. The public understandably considers these to be a bad thing. Economists, however, are less concerned. According to polling among economists, they actually embrace layoffs, because they believe that this means these new workers, who were not needed at their old firm, can turn to new, more productive employment. Many economists also believe that their position is obvious once one acquires adequate economic knowledge. But are they right?[91]

For instance, stress-related illnesses and burnout increase dramatically in firms facing major layoffs. That means even the workers who remain suffer negative consequences. After all, firms may provide goods and services but they do this through employing actual human beings, who suffer things like anxiety, fear, stress, exhaustion, lack of community, a need for teamwork, and so on.[92]

What about the laid off workers? Conventional economic theory says that they will find work that is more productive and efficient for the economy. But is this true in reality? They may in fact struggle to find any new work and if they do it may well be worse in terms of pay, benefits, security, and status. In the real world economies do not immediately and perfectly shift resources to their most efficient locations. Even if they do this in the long term, it is hard to justify the massive suffering caused in the present. As Keynes noted, in the long run we are all dead. Real people need economic practices that help them in the here and now, with rent, medical bills, student loans, and so on. Finally, efficiently shifting production does not necessarily create more good jobs. If one labor-intensive firm lays off 4,000 workers and a new, more efficient IT firm hires 500 workers, the economy, *from a labor standpoint*, has not improved. This is not just hypothetical: there is considerable evidence that this fairly characterizes many of the changes facing the US and other advanced economies in recent decades. The upshot is that many formerly middle-class workers slip down into low-paying, insecure service sector jobs.

There is good reason to think that this applies to a range of issues. Survey data indicates that the public disagrees with professional economists on many areas of economic importance. Contrary to what economists think, which is that the public are systematically misguided, the answer may very well be the opposite, for reasons similar to those mentioned above. A rich, holistic under-standing of the world, which includes but is not limited to the quantitative data economists focus on, may lead us to recognize that the public does have experiential knowledge that challenges many long-held assumptions among professional economists.[93] For instance, the public is much more likely than economists to think that cor-porate downsizing, trade agreements, and high executive pay are problematic.[94] They may well be correct.

Matt Stoller offers an example of the recent blind-ness of professional economists regarding trade with China, noting that "You could see this very clearly in the mid-2000s, when millions of people were saying 'Hey, you're moving our jobs to China, we don't like that.' Economists didn't think that was true until 2011 or so, when three econo-mists wrote a paper called *The China Shock*. All of a sudden, economists had 'proven' what millions of people were saying happened. Economists can't see things in real time because they don't listen to people, only to other economists."[95] Again, a clear example of the disconnect between eco-nomic and intellectual elites, on the one hand, and ordinary citizens, on the other. The ordinary citizens were right.

This is in part because the economics profession is obsessed with abstract mathematical models rather than empirical research and qualitative insight. As Thomas Piketty perceptively observes, "the discipline of economics has yet to get over its childish passion for mathematics...this obsession with mathematics is an easy way of acquiring the appearance of scientificity without having to answer the more complex problems posed by the world we live in."[96] Similarly, Dan Drezner has argued that economists have been prominent and successful thought leaders because they combine absolute confidence in simple answers (free markets, free trade) with abstruse mathematical models that awe and befuddle scholars and lay citizens alike, while telling us nothing of value about the real world.[97]

This reaches its most absurd point when economist Bryan Caplan, speaking for many in his profession, accuses the public of having a "make-work" bias. That is, the public is overly focused on *getting a job* and tends "to underestimate the benefits of conserving labor." Given that ordinary people must have a job to acquire the income that allows them to live, it is amazing that they have time to focus on anything else. *Of course* the public is focused on the need for the economy to create good jobs and as individuals on their need to acquire and keep a good job. And frankly, the benefits of conserving labor are overrated. As we have seen in recent decades, when the economy creates low-wage jobs workers must put in *more* hours just to meet their needs and expectations.

For reasons of economic necessity and changes in cultural norms, American workers work more than we used to. We don't sit around and enjoy our gadgets because we can't afford to.

In a world in which a basic income provides economic security and dignity to every citizen, it will make sense to celebrate developments that conserve labor. If and when that happens, the citizenry will likely agree. Until then, we are better off listening to ordinary citizens on the importance of good-paying, secure, respected employment, rather than the economists who claim to speak on their behalf.

Are they realistic? Means tested versus universal social programs

Elitists, among economists, political scientists, and other pundits, often stress the ignorance of citizens in terms of their inability to answer certain factual survey questions, like naming the chief justice of the supreme court. The problem is that such knowledge is not sufficient to being a thoughtful citizen. It may not even be necessary, as I discuss in *Does Democracy Have a Future?* As Paulo Freire notes in his famous *Pedagogy of the Oppressed*, the masses (he is referring to Latin American peasants) often fail to "realize that they too know things they have learned in their relations with the world and with other women and men."[98] Experiential knowledge is something like this.

In response to these points thoughtful elitists like Christopher Achen, Larry Bartels, Jason Brennan, Byran Caplan, and others are forced to acknowledge that these factual survey questions at best serve as a proxy for more substantial knowledge and insight into politics. But what if they don't? What if experiential knowledge is real? What if it provides insights that can't be gained by those on the outside, or that are at the very least difficult to perceive? Citizens have a bias toward jobs because they know that in our political-economic system jobs are necessary for food, shelter, medical care, status, and so on. If this experiential knowledge is real, at least regarding work and the broader economy, it casts doubt on the overconfident elitism of intellectual, political, and economic elites. And if this is so, professional expertise as a justification for elitism becomes less powerful, at least in areas where ordinary people may have more rich experience than experts, and thus more knowledge and understanding.

I therefore close with one final example of the interconnections between elitism, identity, policy preferences, and experiential knowledge.

It is likely that universal social programs (like medicare for all or a universal basic income) are not only more just but also more politically effective—that is, they are more likely to produce political support and votes—than small, means-tested programs that are only available for some segments of the poor.

On a personal level, in several low-wage jobs I have heard many co-workers express various forms of resentment or frustration at the fact that while they work hard, and receive little or no government benefits, others, who work less, or make a little less, do in fact receive benefits. I have even heard coworkers express concerns about the poverty traps that our means-tested programs entail: a fear that if I get a small raise, I might lose my eligibility for food stamps, Medicaid, section 8 housing, welfare, etc...There is good reason to believe that these concerns are widespread among the bottom half of earners in the United States. And unlike the wealthy railing against the poor, working class citizens who are priced out of means-tested programs have legitimate cause to be frustrated.

This is not a racial dog whistle, either. I've personally heard black, white, and latino coworkers express such concerns and it is usually along the lines of a simple concern for material self-interest: "I don't want to lose benefit x because of my small raise..." To be absolutely clear, the working classes comprise all races of Americans and it is the aspiration of democratic populists like Bernie Sanders to unite all these people around a platform of universal social programs such as Medicare for All. That is why, in practical terms, Sanders best represents the populist, democratic, and anti-elitist position advocated here.[99]

So, what can be done about means-tested programs that potentially incentivize workers to not increase their hours and to avoid raises and promotions? First of all, this is an absurd problem, wholly created by a punitive, disciplinary, condescending set of welfare programs. It is in no way necessary or natural. It is simply bad policy. The answer, of course, is not to cut such programs, as conservatives often argue, but rather to make them universal, that is, available to everyone. Universal programs have no stigma and no incentive to reduce one's earnings to maintain benefits. The most prominent examples in the United States of more or less universal programs are Social Security, which is universal for retired workers and Medicare, which is universal for those 65 and older. Notably, they are both the largest and the most popular social programs in the United States.

Second, hard workers of all races have a point. While they work hard, and make very little, they receive little help in turn from the government. They naturally think, "hey, I play by the rules, why are those other people getting benefits?" Even if they are being unsympathetic to the reasons some people might not be able to work (disability, psychological problems, drug addiction, single parenting, and so on), workers are right to ask why they don't get benefits for themselves. Do we really think that someone working a blue-collar job, probably 50 or more hours a week, with 2 or 3 holidays a year, making about $30,000, has an adequate income? Because $30,000 a year is going to price them out of pretty much all means-tested programs.

It is not a huge leap, from this frustration, to the conclusion that social programs only help the lazy poor, rather than the industrious ones, and that they should therefore be cancelled. This is what the Republican Party is advocating. This is partly how they get votes, by combining such complaints with racial dog whistles[100] The better answer is not to eliminate means-tested benefits programs but to transform them into universal ones (and in doing so to appeal to Americans' better aspirations for racial equality).

It should also be noted, among much of the working class and the poor, that these are not overly politicized people. They express these frustrations not from some consistent right-wing ideology but just because that's how things look to them, as they experience the world with their own eyes. As Katherine Cramer notes, "this is a demographic that displays considerable ambivalence about, not solid allegiance to, the Democratic and Republican Parties."[101] These people can be persuaded to vote for those on the left, if offered the right ideas. Many of them, particularly the young, already lean vaguely left. They are, as Ian Haney Lopez notes in his book *Merge Left*, best seen as *persuadables*, that is, citizens who can be persuaded to vote for the left or the right. This is not, however, because they are committed centrists, as the inside-the-beltway crowd likes to think. They are instead often lacking a clear political ideology or are committed to a mix of left and right viewpoints. There is nothing incoherent in such a worldview; rather, we should see these citizens as people who can be pulled to the left or the right depending on what is being offered. They are rightly skeptical of conventional elites but open to the appeals of populist outsiders like Sanders.

Frankly, much of this should be really obvious. And yet, the Democratic Party, and the leading intellectual elements that support it, have spent recent decades advocating for "realistic", means-tested welfare programs. This is also seen today in intra-party disputes among Democrats as the progressive wing of the party is chastised for failing to be "realistic." Means-tested programs are not realistic, however, if realistic means feasible and endurable. They erode support and legitimacy for welfare programs and empower the right-wing. They lead to a loss of votes and popularity. They have helped to drive elements of the working class toward the right, which stands as a remarkable feat. They discredit the left and the good ideas it has, which at their best are bold and powerful.

As Lopez helpfully observes in *Merge Left*, when racial anxiety is used to divide Americans it leads to politicians on the right being elected and to reductions in social programs. In his words, "every racial community loses when too many people vote their racial anxieties."[102] To repeat, the best answer to combat this is not limited, means-tested programs, which too easily connect to racial narratives and are used by elites to divide Americans, no matter how "realistic" they appear to be. The best answer remains universal programs like Medicare for All.

This also demonstrates the insular nature of the Democratic Party, the think tank network that supports it, and its donors. Have any of these people have ever had a working-class job? Have they even met someone who has a working-class job? The answer, for too many of them, is no. These people haven't. In a society with limited class mobility, these professional class writers, staffers, politicians, and donors don't have connections to the working class. They were raised by educated parents and shepherded into the same class themselves. And that, at least partly, explains their cluelessness.[103]

There is a reason Bernie Sanders' "unrealistic" agenda is so appealing to ordinary people. Indeed, his support in the 2019-2020 Democratic presidential primary has largely come from a diverse coalition of young, working class people of all colors. It avoids the problems I have mentioned by demanding that we replace means-tested programs with universal programs. The kind of programs that have widespread legitimacy and don't generate resentment. The only criticism one can level against such programs is that they are expensive. That doesn't have a lot of sting right now.

This again suggests that the day-to-day experiences of ordinary working Americans lend insight into politics that elites all too frequently lack. By listening more to ordinary citizens and giving them more political power we have a chance to better address these issues. The following chapter turns to the academic world, where many of the ideas that feed into the elitist worldview are perpetuated.

CHAPTER FIVE:
THE ACADEMY

In a book centered on discussions of elitism, politics, and knowledge it makes sense to turn to the academic world. Focusing on the American university system can seem like an esoteric exercise, of interest only to full-time professors and other full-time university staff. It would be a mistake to make this assumption. Not only do universities play a large role in American life and the formation and perpetuation of elite rule but they also are an increasingly universal experience for Americans, particularly younger ones. A full two-thirds of American adults attend some college these days. It is not only in professional class bubbles that university attendance is a common aspiration and occurrence.

The problems, however, are many. Only about one-third of American adults have a bachelor's degree. The specific numbers vary year to year but the basic takeaway is that many Americans, perhaps a majority who attend college, do not graduate. There are all sorts of reasons for this, many of them class-based. Many middle and working class students struggle with hefty tuition payments and many poor students, who in principle qualify for substantial financial aid, lack the training, social capital, and connections to get into college in the first place. Financial aid, even full tuition coverage, is of course no help to those who don't attend college.

The academy therefore matters because it is increasingly part of the life experience of many Americans, even if only for a few years, and because it plays a central role in the perpetuation not just of intellectual elites but also in the production of economic and political elites.

Although this chapter is titled "The Academy" it can be misleading to treat higher education as one undifferentiated mass. It can be divided into elite research colleges, both public and private; elite liberal arts colleges; state teaching colleges; other small colleges; for-profit colleges; and community colleges. Each of these is distinct in their own way and one could draw the dividing lines differently. To simplify, it will help to at least remember that American universities can be divided into those in which professors are paid primarily to conduct research and those in which professors are paid primarily to teach. Sometimes these distinctions matter greatly for the educational experience of undergraduates, sometimes they do not. The conclusion then ties these threads back into the broader political and economic themes of the book.

Here I explain how the academic world, particularly the most prestigious universities, maintains a system of elite credentialing for the wealthy while also exploiting an increasing number of its own employees so as to save labor costs and shift power to management. This chapter thus challenges several myths regarding the academy: its meritocratic nature, its role in promoting the public good, and its methods for assessing the quality of scholarship. It also engages with arguments that defend the inequality and elitism of higher-ed, including the growing use of adjuncts. I draw on my own experience as an adjunct professor to lend insight into this problem before connecting it to the broader problems of the academy and the economy as a whole.

This chapter is split into two sections. The first focuses on the nature of academic scholarship, the academic job market, elite bias in the academic world, and the overproduction of PhDs. The second section shifts the focus to the use of adjunct professors and the changing culture of higher education. I aim to show that these issues matter not just for scholars but for the broader public and their sometimes fleeting connections to university life. The chapter concludes with a brief appendix on the role of "postmodern" thought within the academy and its relation to other political developments.

Elite bias, scholarship, and the overproduction of PhDs

In recent years many scholars, journalists, and other commentators have highlighted the way in which America's universities have changed over the past few decades. Much of this has rightly focused on the increase in adjunct faculty relative to tenure-track faculty and the corporate takeover of the university in terms of guiding ideology, managerial dominance, and labor relations, in addition to the marketing of universities as companies providing a service to would-be consumers (what we used to call students). I endorse this critique, particularly the focus on the takeover of the university system by a highly-paid managerial class, steeped in corporate values, and the decline in the percentage of professors on the tenure-track. (Most current estimates put the percentage of faculty in contingent positions north of 70%). Declining public funding for universities (on a per-student basis), the rise of a boated managerial class, and expensive amenities have all contributed to an explosive growth in university tuition expenses, which harm millions of Americans.

I want to sketch out a few distinct thoughts here. The aforementioned critiques focus on how a management class has taken over American universities and recreated them in a corporate, neoliberal image. This is largely not the fault of the faculty; indeed, many have resisted this takeover. There are, however, aspects of disfunction and injustice within the faculty-dominated academic side of the university that still deserve mentioning, particularly out of respect for current and prospective graduate students as well as the broader citizenry who must reside in this elite-dominated world. These problems directly relate to the various forms of elitism discussed above.

What are the problems with elite bias in the academic world? First of all, PhD students at research universities are led to believe, by their professors, school administrators, and the broader academic culture, that professorships are distributed on the basis of merit. They are told, in other words, that publications, research grants, and teaching awards are the distinguishing marks that will enable the best of them to rise to the top and secure the best faculty positions. This has little relation to the truth. Good jobs (i.e. all tenure-track jobs, particularly at prestigious R1 universities and liberal arts colleges, in addition to competitive postdocs and other temporary research positions) are distributed largely on the basis of three factors: the conventional prestige of one's PhD-granting university, the reputation and influence of one's advisor, and a large dose of luck. None of these have any relation to the efforts that graduate students make to distinguish themselves as successful scholars or impressive teachers.

This matters because it means that undergraduates are not necessarily taught by the best (however we might define it) but rather by the best-connected. It also means that efforts to challenge the elitism of the academy will not be fruitful. Those with perspectives and life-experiences distinct from predominant intellectual elites are unlikely to find a place in the upper-tiers of the university system.

Consider the following: the University of California system includes nine major public research universities and several medical schools, among many other facilities. Several of these, UC Berkeley, UCLA, and UC San Diego, for example, are among the most conventionally prestigious universities in the world, frequently ranked alongside famous private universities like Harvard, Stanford, and the University of Chicago. Several others, like UC Davis, UC Irvine, and UC Santa Barbara, are recognized as world-class institutions. Several more, UC Santa Cruz and UC Riverside, for instance, are well-regarded up and coming universities. The system is, by any measure, a prestigious and desirable place for an aspiring academic to secure a tenure-track job. This makes it all the more significant that such jobs are largely reserved for graduates of the most highly ranked graduate programs.

For instance, conducting an informal count in my discipline of political science, I found that approximately 85% of all tenure-track professors in political science departments across the University of California system received their PhD at a top-15 political science program, as rated by *US News and World Report*. Given the ongoing nature of academic hiring, these exact numbers will of course vary from year to year. The point is that they illustrate bluntly the elite nature of academic hiring. The majority of schools in the University of California system grant PhDs in political science but only three (Berkeley, Los Angeles, and San Diego) consistently rank in the top 15 nationally. Therefore students receiving a PhD from the Irvine, Riverside, Santa Barbara, Santa Cruz, and Davis campuses will find it bordering on impossible to obtain a tenure-track job in the University of California system, even though they are receiving a degree from that very system! (Imagine what would happen if PhD students were told this upfront when applying and again throughout their first year in graduate school).

Furthermore, it is not as if the remaining 15% of tenure-track hires in these political science departments are coming from second-tier political science programs. Many of them are coming from small, boutique departments that, while not ranked in the top 15 nationally, have an elite reputation in a particular subfield of study, like the University of Rochester's focus on public choice and formal theory or Johns Hopkins University's focus on political theory.

Perhaps this is because the overwhelming majority of PhDs are granted by top-15 programs? Alas, this is not so. (There is a case to be made that non-elite PhD programs either should not exist or should be much more explicit about their placement records with prospective and incoming graduate students). But perhaps the PhD students graduating from the top-15 programs are just better? This is not easy to measure (how are we to define "better") and there does not appear to be systematic research on this topic. By at least one metric, publications, there is no reason to think that top-15 program graduates are particularly impressive. Publications are neither a necessary nor a sufficient condition for acquiring a good academic job. Every discipline is filled with stories of students graduating from top-tier programs without any publications and moving directly into prestigious postdocs and tenure-track jobs. Similarly, many students from second-tier PhD programs who have successfully published in well-regarded peer-reviewed journals find themselves stuck as adjunct professors. As various research has confirmed, the best way to acquire a good academic job is *not* through publications or teaching experience; rather, it is through having an influential advisor while being enrolled at a top-tier program.

Why does this matter? First, because it is unfair. Elitism and nepotism are widely regarded as illegitimate means for distributing spoils, be they jobs, status, resources, or other things of value. Furthermore, at least publicly, both elites and regular citizens in all realms of life in America denounce nepotism. Yet it is an accurate characterization of this self-reinforcing elitism in the academy. Phrases like "networking" and "connections" are euphemisms for nepotism, used precisely because nepotism is regarded as illegitimate.

These practices are also deceptive. They play on the sense students have of their own worth—most graduate students were hard-working, successful undergraduates who were indeed able to distinguish themselves on the basis of skill in the classroom. They believe that they will do so again in graduate school and are told as much for the duration of their studies. To find out, after years on the job market, that such skills have little to do with landing a good job, is not only disheartening but emotionally crushing and infuriating. Every year, hundreds, if not thousands, of recent PhDs discover, after spending the better part of their 20s or 30s foregoing other income and educational opportunities, that the rules they were told to adhere to (publish, publish, publish!) are not in fact the rules that allocate good jobs (go to

Harvard, have a famous advisor, be lucky!). Lest this seem too narrow a concern, the conclusion connects this problem to broader problems in the economy.[104]

If university elitism regarding the value of various degrees, combined with the personal nepotism of influential individual advisors, guides the acquisition of a good job, the acquisition of tenure then does a dramatic 180 degree shift. Having acquired a tenure-track job, the newly hired professor discovers that the path to tenure does indeed rely on excelling in the areas that the university claims to value (teaching for some colleges, research for others). For state teaching colleges and community colleges, this makes sense. New professors are assessed in terms of their teaching ability, measured through student evaluations, department assessments, and other metrics. Even so, such teachers are generally underpaid, heavily overworked, and forced into burnout and exhaustion from having to teach so many courses. In cases where they don't have the help of teaching assistants, professors are forced to rely on multiple-choice tests and to cut corners wherever possible. And of course this leaves little time or energy for research and original thinking. The same story goes for the contingent faculty, with every difficulty heightened considerably.

When it comes to tenure-track jobs at research universities, the publish or perish ethos takes hold once the job is acquired. This is also troubling. First, tenure-track professors at research universities are strongly encouraged, both formally and informally, to minimize and even shirk their teaching duties, putting as little thought and energy into them as possible. They are, however, encouraged to publish. So is this good? Once someone has acquired a tenure-track job at a research university they are required to engage in research to advance in their career. How could this be a problem?

The basic point to make is that professors at research universities are rewarded for output, not research. But what, exactly, is the difference? In a hyper-specialized, overworked academic world, the quantity of articles and books, combined with an assessment of the conventional prestige of the publisher, serves as a proxy for the actual quality of the work. But these are indeed different standards and they need to be understood as such. Careful, thoughtful, quality research is not rewarded, particularly if it takes a long time (and we should expect that it will be time-consuming). A lengthy, ambitious, original research project undertaken pre-tenure is a guarantee that one will fail to receive tenure. Churning out a giant quantity of articles and books, on the other hand, is a guarantee of tenure.[105] As Frank Donoghue notes in *The Last Professors*, "the market categories of productivity, efficiency, and competitive achievement, not

intelligence or erudition, already drive professional advancement in the academic world, even
in the humanities."[106]

This pressure to churn out publications that are
seen to be prestigious and cutting-edge (without
necessarily being so) also impacts the physical
and natural sciences in troubling ways. There is a
growing problem of replicability within the sciences, because new research that reports a novel,
exciting finding is more likely to be published
in a major journal, more likely to receive academic accolades and favorable media coverage,
more likely to elicit current and future grant
money, and more likely to advance one's career.
The problem, of course, is that without regular
attempts to replicate scientific findings we have
good reason to doubt the accuracy of the results.
What does cutting-edge laboratory work tell us if
other labs, with similar data and techniques, cannot replicate the results? And why try replication,
given that it promises nothing in the way of career advancement?[107] These problems may seem
internal to academic culture but they impact
the broader society. We all benefit, and the public good is served, when quality research is conducted, well-funded, and replicated across many
laboratories.

In sum, the elitism of the academy, not only perpetuated by those at the top of the hierarchy
but internalized by those on the lower rungs

of the ladder, is shameful, anti-democratic, and dishonest, given the formally meritocratic ethos of academia. The standards for acquiring tenure, however, are also troubling for a different set of reasons. Fundamentally, the frenetic pace of contemporary academic life, the need to conference, network, self-promote, and either publish incessantly or teach incessantly, all make for a terrible environment in which to engage in careful research, rigorous thought, and original scholarship.

The obvious rejoinder that there are countless articles and books being published is not, in fact, a rebuttal at all. As I hinted at above, the overproduction of academic scholarship is not a sign of a healthy research environment. The widely noted fact that the majority of published articles are never cited is absolutely shocking, though it is never reported as such. As university libraries cut their purchases of academic books, there are literally no readers or buyers for the majority of academic scholarship. Why are we writing these essays and books? The answer, as Donoghue recognizes, is that "publication is the profession's only universally recognized marker of distinction. The glut of publications and planned publications renders the actual content of the books and articles almost insignificant."[108] At this point, much of academic scholarship functions more like a term paper—an act that requires the author to acquire and demonstrate a certain level of knowledge but without the expectation of an audience. If there is no audience for so much of this work, at least we can hope that the authors learn something from the exercise.

What can be done about this frankly absurd situation? For starters, there should probably be much less published academic scholarship. To be clear, this does not mean that it should be more difficult to publish an article. Academic elitism, combined with the groupthink characteristic of any domain of human life, suggests that a smaller number of journals will not necessarily winnow out the weakest scholarship or produce the most innovative research. What I am suggesting is that professors should write far fewer things intended for publication. Many articles don't need to be published and many other articles don't need to be expanded into bloated books. This, again, is not an attack on articles or books. It is a suggestion that professional advancement should not be judged by the quantity of output published by a scholar. How to institutionalize such a change, both in the formal requirements for getting and keeping a job, and in the informal culture of the academy, is a much harder question to answer. A successful answer would, however, benefit not just professors and graduate students but undergraduates and the broader public as well. Let me close with a suggestion for what this could look like in practice.

Universities should dramatically expand their hiring of faculty for tenure-track or equivalent positions.[109] Adjuncts and other contingent faculty should see their positions turned into full-time, tenure-track positions. This will not solve all of the problems mentioned above, many of which are internal to academic culture, particularly with regard to its persistent elitism. But more faculty, particularly when they are properly compensated, means fewer students per class, lighter teaching loads per professor, more energy and attention to devote to individual student needs, and more energy, time, and attention to devote to careful research and writing.

Forget for a second the short-term political constraints on such changes. Picture instead the university as it should be: fairly remunerated professors, secure in their positions, able to devote considerable energy and innovation to a small number of courses, attend to their students' needs, and conduct research at their desired pace. No frenetic running from one class to the next, no racing up and down the interstate to make your next teaching appointment, no pressure to forget about your 100 students and focus on the dozens of articles you need to write to acquire tenure. On the student side, imagine a university in which classes are smaller, learning is less rote, education is more tailored to your passions and interests, and professors know your name and have a personal stake in your success. Imagine a world in which those professors are able to give you detailed feedback on every assignment, without fail (or exhaustion on their part) because they are not bogged down with an impossible number of students. This would be education "as the development of individuals who will be able to practice the life of free citizens."[110] This is what a university should look like. Now we have to figure out how to get there.

Adjuncts, administrators, and the changing culture of higher ed

As a bridging point that connects inequality to experimental knowledge and elitism, I conclude with some of the effects of rampant inequality on higher education. In their book *Cracks in the Ivory Tower: The Moral Mess of Higher Education,* Jason Brennan and Philip Magness offer a number of criticisms of higher ed in America. Although they make several interesting and original points, there are some glaring problems with the text. First, they largely ignore the fact that America's elite universities serve to perpetuate an entrenched elite class of privileged citizens. (In recent years upwards of half of all incoming students at Harvard, Princeton, and Yale have been legacies. Not to mention the large number of graduates from such schools who will go on to work in finance on Wall Street). Second, although they briefly discuss the problem of adjunct professorship, they largely ignore it and indeed dismiss the problem of adjunct pay, job security, and benefits, as a non-issue. As I will show, however, the problem of adequate pay, benefits, and job security is of concern to large majorities of Americans. What is happening in our universities reflects society-wide trends.

Brennan and Magness' brief discussion of adjunct professors in America is presented with a few facts in a straightforward, friendly manner and the reader is left wondering how to square these authors' largely comforting assessment of the use of adjunct professors with the lived experience of those who have in fact been adjuncts. Their account can seem innocuous (if misguided) at first glance but upon further reflection it is quite problematic.

To begin with, adjunct professors are those who are teaching college classes but doing so on a contingent, class-by-class basis. The pay is often remarkably low (sometimes $1500 or less per class) and benefits are often non-existent. It is generally, and correctly, regarded as a problem that many of the professors teaching our students (as many as 70%) are poorly paid, overworked, insecure employees. It matters not just for their livelihoods but also for the quality of education provided to American students.

So why are Brennan and Magness so sanguine about the problem? What are they up to? First of all, Brennan and Magness try to assess whether adjunct professors are underpaid (a much more complex question than they grant). Doing so, they compare two hypothetical professors who have similar resumes: a tenure-track assistant professor at a teaching intensive college and an adjunct professor with a similar teaching load. On their account, the tenure-track professor, with benefits included, earns approximately $30 an hour (their account of hours worked by the two professors is far from convincing, particularly regarding the adjunct). The adjunct, on the other hand, earns about $20 an hour. They seem to think this is not a big difference.

In itself this is a shocking assessment, truly incomprehensible how Oxford University Press reviewers and publishers let them get away with such a judgment. These are *massively* different pay scales. Just mathematically, this typical, hypothetical teaching professor with a tenure-track job is earning approximately 50% more than the adjunct professor for similar work and hours. This is literally tens of thousands of dollars of income, per year, more for the tenure-track professor. People fight and scrape their entire lives to get raises like that. This "small" difference is an enormous one that working class citizens put in years of loyal service with a firm to achieve. Now consider Brennan and Magness' version of the story: "adjuncts make less total money than comparable teaching-intensive professors because they work less and do less, not because they get paid much less per hour spent teaching."[111] They present their work in a colloquial fashion, so let's join them. Their account is bullshit.

But let's grant them every assumption they make: given an assumption that vastly underestimates the number of hours adjuncts work, they suggest the per-hour pay disparity between tenure-track and adjunct professors could be as little as four dollars ($24 per hour for the tenure-track in their first year, $20 per hour for the adjunct). Again, let's accept that this is correct (and ignore the fact that the tenure-track faculty will see substantial yearly pay increases, while the adjunct won't, so they are showing the scenario in which the two incomes are the closest that they will ever be. The authors incorrectly present it as something of the opposite). Four dollars per hour is still a large difference in pay, particularly over the course of multiple years. We are talking thousands more dollars per year for the tenure-track professor. And this is granting the assumptions of Brennan and Magness, which we don't have to (I will discuss a few below).

It is also not necessary to compare the pay of the adjunct to a first year professor. After ten years (or twenty, and so on), the adjunct pay will rise little, if at all, whereas the tenure-track professor will see substantial pay increases, with the potential for their yearly salary to double over a lifetime of work. So adjuncts can rightly point to the higher pay of more senior professors, who have received pay increases that are not available to the adjunct, even if she puts in similar years of work. Focusing on first-year professors is a sleight of hand, drawing attention to the year in which the pay of adjunct and tenure-track professors will be closest while ignoring the yawning gap that will emerge over time.

But why does this matter for the broader political conversation? Frankly, it matters because it shows what happens in a deeply unequal society. Those with good incomes, and that includes professionals with comfortable six-figure incomes and status, not just billionaires, have a tendency to not only justify their position but to downplay the challenges and struggles of those below them. No surprise, for they might feel guilty if they didn't. This very much includes college professors and administrators, even many liberal ones. To put it bluntly: anyone who works a low-income job knows that every single dollar matters. A four dollar per hour discrepancy in starting pay, with substantial opportunities for growth going to the higher paid employee, is a big deal. But some Americans, including these authors, are making too much to notice or care. They aren't alone.

It also matters because it reflects a problematic change in America's universities that parallels changes in every other industry. America, with decades of growing inequality, is increasingly a winner-take-all society, in which a small number of people receive excellent pay, status, and benefits, and the majority struggle to make ends meet. Adjunct professors are the university version of this. They are the result of universities becoming more like corporations, simultaneously seeking to cut labor costs (through the use of adjuncts) and expand their bloated managerial class of employees.[112]

Since Brennan and Magness tackle many of these issues, let's look closer at some of their assumptions, for they help us see how the powerful (political, economic, and intellectual elites) see the world and justify their power and influence. First, focusing on dollar per hour pay, rather than yearly income, is an effective rhetorical move. $30 versus $20? That doesn't sound so bad. $24 versus $20? That's nothing. But of course we aren't talking about these numbers. We are talking about how they accumulate over the course of weeks, months, and years. Note that Brennan and Magness don't talk about *years,* in which case the tenure-track faculty earns tens of thousands more in income per year, *every year*. Now add that up over a lifetime and you see why adjuncts want better pay. The same story applies to all low and medium wage workers across the economy.

It also lends insight into how inequality compounds over time. Poor and working class Americans, who comprise at least half of the country, use their entire incomes to pay for necessities. They don't save because they can't—every last dollar is needed to cover living expenses. The professional classes, on the other hand, are able to save thousands each year. The top one percent even more so. This leads to a situation where, as mentioned above, a majority of Americans don't have $400 available for an emergency while a small subset have thousands, tens of thousands, or even millions saved. Some Americans are literally worth billions. Let these discrepancies sink in. It is no surprise that political, economic, and intellectual elites are frequently oblivious to the lives of ordinary citizens.

Returning to the theme of this chapter, let's see how intellectual and economic elites work to justify their position. As I have stressed, this example of underpaid adjunct professors is illustrative of larger, ongoing economic trends. Adjuncts are not unique but rather part of the broader working class. This is why they matter.

Brennan and Magness make another important rhetorical move that must be observed. They stress that many adjunct professors only teach part time. These are professionals with other good jobs who occasionally teach a class here or there. But this is an irrelevant distraction. Those fighting for better adjunct pay and benefits are not worried about employees at think tanks or the federal government who occasionally teach a course at Georgetown or George Mason. Or consider the following hypothetical example: if Stephen King teaches a course on creative writing, that is all well and good (it sounds fun!) but, correctly, nobody cares about his pay for the course, unless it is obscenely high. We certainly aren't worried about him being underpaid. What those who speak and act on behalf of adjuncts are demanding is better pay, benefits, and job security for the adjunct professors who are teaching many courses and trying to make a living. They tend to have PhDs from highly ranked programs, with considerable teaching experience and peer-reviewed publications. Indeed, in my experience we are almost exclusively talking about such people. So why bring up the irrelevant, non-exploited "adjuncts"? You tell me.

Also consider, Brennan and Magness don't discuss the pay of research professors other than to note the obvious fact that they are paid more highly than faculty at teaching-intensive colleges. But research faculty are very much part of the adjunct story. Those advocating on behalf of adjunct professors are not focusing our ire on the lowest paid tenure-track professors at teaching colleges, who while benefiting from tenure are still generally overworked and underpaid. We are focusing just as much on overpaid professors at research universities, where it is hard to see how their high six-figure incomes are justified other than in tautological terms (like those who claim these high incomes reflect their market value, for instance). But how to defend a system in which research professors frequently earn between $100,000 and $300,000 or more per year while adjuncts, often with similar credentials, work full time for fractions of that pay? Can it really be that their research is so much more socially beneficial? This may be true for some number of people in the medical sciences, and here and there in other disciplines, but it surely isn't true for most of them.[113] How, for instance, does writing a book that justifies the painfully low pay and precarity of their adjunct colleagues serve anyone other than tenured research professors? An important point made by those speaking on behalf of adjuncts is that it would be better if the incomes of the top half of full-time professors were reduced and the incomes of the bottom half correspondingly increased. This would help adjuncts, visiting professors, postdocs, lecturers, and lower income tenure-track professors at the expense of the best off tenured research professors.

More broadly, many aspects of the adjunct experience can't be easily quantified but they are integral to it, as anyone who has been an adjunct knows. How do you quantity the massive loss of status, job security, and free time spent applying to other jobs? This is something adjuncts more or less have to do, whereas one could argue that when tenure-track and tenured professors apply to other jobs it is at least partly a voluntary activity. And time applying to jobs cannot be quantified just in hours. It also involves stress, despair, and pain searching for low-probability jobs. It also hurts to feel oneself a failure. As psychologists and public health researchers have shown, these things have tangible consequences for physical and mental health. It is no exaggeration to say that most high-status, high-income professors (and others with similar occupations) literally have no idea what such feelings are like. They have not experienced them in any sustained manner. The psychological distress resulting from unemployment, underemployment, and precarity is nevertheless a fraught, lived reality for the majority.

Again, these problems are not limited to adjunct professors but rather experienced by millions of underpaid Americans struggling to make ends meet while the majority of the economy's resources are concentrated at the top.

There are many other points we could address in the authors' assumptions: they ignore the course prep-time in between quarters and semesters when adjuncts are not paid but are very much working, by preparing their upcoming courses. They also mention that tenure-track professors have service obligations while ignoring the fact that it is common practice at many universities for professors to take on service obligations in exchange for reduced teaching loads. This happens at both teaching and research universities. It is an interesting omission, for ask any adjunct and they would probably happily trade a course or two for some well-compensated time spent in university service. One could go on. The broad point to make is that their assumptions regarding adjunct work hours are deeply unsympathetic and severely underestimate the number of hours adjuncts work. It is truly a great testament to the general thrust of the arguments I am making that these authors are so glaringly out of touch: they think they are being charitable by possibly *overestimating* how hard it is to be an adjunct. They are unaware of the things I have mentioned because they are not adjuncts and they are not around adjuncts. This is a slight taste of how elitism (and being an elite) works, how it yields conformity and closed-mindedness, and a frankly embarrassing ignorance of reality. But bubbles sure are cozy.[114]

Brennan and Magness also note that adjuncts aren't paid to do research, so that this is not a job requirement. While technically true, this is deeply misleading. Adjuncts aren't paid by their universities to do research but it is still often experienced as a requirement. To stay a part of their profession, adjuncts frequently need to attend conferences, network, research and publish, and attempt to participate in department and university activities, even though they are not compensated for such activity. Unlike professors with job security and a good salary, who can afford to spend a summer researching, an adjunct will make no income unless teaching. It is thus very difficult to find the time or energy to do research, even though it is necessary as the best chance young adjuncts have of advancing to a better position. They will thus often have to teach more classes in the summer, or take on other work, just to pay the bills. This keeps them in the adjunct trap, hoping for and being qualified for better jobs but unable to get them, and without the time or energy to be productive researchers. All of these activities are effectively work activities, even if uncompensated.

Adjuncts also often engage in mentoring and other activities to help their students. Sure, they could say, "nope, I'm not paid for this" but they tend to be idealistic teachers and good people, and thus do it as part of their professional responsibility. Again, uncompensated work hours. Those dismissive of adjunct concerns might call them dupes. But wouldn't it be more respectable for faculty to use their position of power to advocate for better pay, benefits, and job security for adjuncts, rather than telling them to minimize their work hours, lower their quality of work, and maximize their hourly pay? "Reduce your work load by shirking your teaching duties" is pretty bad advice to give to any teacher, anywhere.[115] And yet it is implicit in many defenses of the current adjunct system.

So a really important takeaway from this discussion is that adjuncts, teaching professors, and research professors are in practice part of the same profession. They have similar graduate training and often have similar aspirations. They all, to varying degrees, engage in teaching, research, and service. They are de facto much more similar than Brennan and Magness allow. But it is in the self-interest of tenured research professors to ignore this point because they want to justify their privileged position in academia. If all scholars are part of the same academic family, the winner-take-all academic world in which high incomes, grants, and status go to a small number of scholars is not justified. We should not celebrate but lament the "creation of a university culture that has increasingly become a glittering world of superstars, supersalaries, and technical competence."[116]

I belabor these points because I want to challenge Brennan and Magness' assumptions. They think that the disparity between adjunct and beginning tenure track pay might be lower if they assumed adjuncts work less. I have tried to show adjuncts work more than the authors give them credit for. They also fail to note that it is in the nature of teaching that the hours spent per class are not fixed. Teaching can balloon to take almost unlimited amounts of time. A tenure-track professor with 4 classes and service responsibilities might work the same hours as an adjunct with 4 classes and no service. Partly for the reasons enumerated above, partly because there are only so many hours in the week and there are upper bounds to how much people can work. The overworked tenure track professor will feel a bit of squeeze in her classes and maybe spend a little less time on each. The adjunct, with less squeeze, may spend a little more time on each class. This isn't being a dupe. It is being a good teacher. Put differently, the hours spent per week per class tend to go down as the number of classes taught, number of students, and number of other responsibilities go up. So the authors' comparisons are not great, again in ways that understate how tough it is to be an adjunct.

We also might note in passing the laughable claim the authors make that the introductory classes taught by adjuncts are easier than the upper-division ones sometimes taught by tenure track professors. Seriously? Teaching a required introductory course to students who don't want to be there, are less interested, know less, give worse reviews, and whom there are more of, and thus more time spent grading, is easier than teaching your pet upper-level class to a smaller number of smart, motivated upperclassmen? Give me a break. On this logic, our hearts should bleed for professors at prestigious PhD-granting schools for the grad seminars they get to/have to teach. The poor souls, they must suffer so! Later in their book (chapter 8), the authors reverse course and make points similar to my own, conceding that introductory classes are in general the least enjoyable to teach.

Again, the importance of these developments lies not just in their significance for the American university system. They are indicative of broader political and economic trends in which gains in income, security, and status are concentrated among a handful of (supposedly meritocratic) winners and precarity, low-wages, low status, and limited benefits are concentrated among the vast majority. These changes are happening in America's universities because they are happening everywhere.

One could write an entire book on the changing nature of the modern university system in America (several have).[117] This chapter concludes on a short note regarding these changes. Writing in the 1980s, Sheldon Wolin, without using the word neoliberalism, reflected on the growth of corporate values in the university system (and the broader public sphere), claiming that "the private realm has invaded the public."[118] He elaborates: "in light of the close integration of public and corporate policies and the cooperation that exists today between state officials and corporate representatives, the old dichotomies between the political state and the private economy are anachronistic."[119]

Brennan and Magness, for instance, are dubious about claims that neoliberalism has overtaken the academy. But they offer little analysis other than pointing to the number of professors and administrators who self-identify as liberal. This is an irrelevant point, however. In the works of thoughtful scholars like Wendy Brown, David Harvey, William Connolly, and others,[120] neoliberalism refers to a process in which market ideas, relations, practices, and institutions take over an increasing number of spheres of life. It has nothing to do with being liberal or conservative in the American sense. Indeed, since the 1980s and 1990s the majority of American elites, conservative, centrist, and liberal, have been *neoliberal* in this broader sense. They have embraced, as Joseph Stiglitz terms it, a "market fundamentalist" worldview and sought to expand this to all domains of human life. In this sense, Wolin, prescient as always, was correct decades ago in identifying the "near-totality in which public and private distinctions are being steadily blurred."[121] Understanding this is key to understanding the changing nature of universities, both public and private, as well as the broader unraveling of the American compact.

The conclusion connects these changes in American universities to the broader economy regarding questions of fairness and elitism.

Appendix to Chapter Five: Postmodernism in the Academy

Since at least the 1990s there have been prominent debates, within the academy and in the broader public sphere, over the influence that "postmodern" scholars and styles of thought have had on university life. Some of these debates formed a substantial component of 1990s culture wars. In this appendix I want to offer some brief thoughts on these topics.

More recently, some commentators have blamed postmodern thinking in the academy for the new rise of Trump-era post-truth discourse. In recent work William Connolly responds, I think correctly, that there is an important difference between postmodern scholars critiquing standard Western methods of assessing truth and knowledge, and the outright, proud, defiant lying that defines so much of the Trump movement.[122]

At the same time, there is a different critique to be

made of postmodernism in the academy. Whereas for the past 50-plus years, the right has funded think tanks, both national and local, and all sorts of research and advocacy in the public sphere to propagate their ideas, many on the left went into the academy and engaged in esoteric postmodern debates about the nature of truth and reality.

Now there is nothing wrong, as such, with those debates. But when lots of talented, left-leaning thinkers are engaged in abstract epistemological debates, but think they are contributing to a left-wing political project, we have a problem. Compare what those scholars were doing to what the right has been doing for decades. The right's advocacy is much more political, and effective, than the other. The right's advocacy has also been aimed at the public, not at an insular academic community.[123]

And even now the left isn't really catching up to the right. There are some good think tanks for liberals and those further on the left but they mostly do narrow policy research. Part of the brilliance of the right has been that it has also given room to visionaries. People like Friedrich Von Hayek and James Buchanan, for instance, were more theorists and visionaries than economists. Milton Friedman was both. The prominent liberal think tank Center for American Progress, for instance, doesn't hire visionaries, they hire narrow policy analysts. But the two are complementary and both necessary for impacting public discourse.

Effectively summarizing this point, political theorist Romand Coles recognizes that "while most
of the democratic left has missed this aspect of
political life, the right wing has invested its time,
money, and organized efforts across a wide array
of resonant venues with great success."[124]

My project, as well as many of the works cited
here, represents an effort to contribute to public
debate rather than retreat into the insularity of
the academy.

CHAPTER SIX: CONCLUSION

The preceding chapters have been concerned with different dimensions of elitism and how elite rule has a devastating political, economic, and intellectual impact on America. In this conclusion I explicitly tie the discussion of precarious adjunct labor from chapter five into the rise of insecure, poorly paid, low-status labor that has come to characterize the careers of more and more Americans. This is in part a story about questions of fairness. We might say that the elites who have more or less run our politics, economy, and academic world for the past forty years have violated the implicit contract they had with us, the citizenry. They have not acted fairly—they are in violation of this contract, which we can call the American Compact.

Much has been written on the rise of adjunct labor at American universities and the transformation of our universities into entities concerned with branding, labor costs, and other corporate imperatives. Here I will tie together some of the strands of this book, situating the adjunct faculty experience within the broader context of work in contemporary America. In doing so I hope to shed light on long-term, ongoing political and economic trends in the country, particular the unraveling of the American Compact.

The American Compact is fundamentally about fairness. This compact can be divided into three different compacts, but each is related and they are simultaneously unraveling. They can be loosely defined as follows, based on the level of education one has: The high school compact—if you work hard, you can get a good job, enjoy a reasonable if modest standard of living and with two such incomes, support a family. Even if your job is tough, you can get a secure retirement, save some money, and maybe your kids can have a better future. The college compact—if you get a college degree, you can get a good, upper-middle class job, live a secure and fulfilling life, and have your kids do even better. The graduate school compact—if you get a graduate degree, you can expect a creative, rewarding professional career that is also well-compensated and secure. This compact held, more or less, from the end of World War II until sometime in the mid-to-late 1970s. By 1980 the Compact was thrown out and a new order instated, one of unremitting elite rule at the expense of everyone else. We do not have to be naive about the compact (for instance, it excluded many women and people of color) to recognize that something important has happened in the past four decades, an unraveling that has harmed more and more working Americans of all colors.

This is of course an over-simplification, but it is not an exaggeration to say that all three elements of the compact are currently unwinding. The first has been unraveling for quite some time and the second and third are increasingly doing so as well. The employment situation (good income, benefits, security) is eroding for all three groups.[125] In the meantime, our winner-take-all economy concentrates income, wealth, and status in a tiny class of elites.

The unraveling of the American compact helps to explain why the centers of gravity in American politics, particularly its two main political parties, are collapsing and simultaneously why the populist left and right are increasing in popularity. The collapse of the high school compact helps to explain why so many middle aged and older Americans supported and continue to support Donald Trump. What has been less discussed is how the ongoing collapse of the college and grad school compact led so many Americans in their 20s and 30s to support Bernie Sanders in the Democratic primary in 2016. In addition, in the 2019-2020 Democratic primary Sanders has drawn in a mixture of educated, young Americans and less-educated working class Americans of all ages and races. By focusing on these trends we can gain insight into why Americans have so little faith in our major political and economic institutions and why we are increasingly looking for outsiders to resolve our persistent problems. The simultaneous and interlocking collapse of all three compacts has led to a shocking loss of legitimacy on the part of the major institutions of American political life. It is imperative that we acknowledge this if we are to have any hope of understanding what the future may hold.

Adjunct Professors and the Graduate School Compact
In the previous chapter I discussed the growing use of contingent, low-pay adjunct faculty at American universities and its relation to broader problems with elitism. Here I will expand on that discussion by more explicitly drawing on my own experience. This in turn will let me connect it to the more general problems that I have diagnosed.

To lay all the cards on the table, my adjunct experience was better than most. I earned a PhD in the University of California system and spent two years teaching in the Cal State system, which thanks to a strong faculty union has negotiated good benefits for adjunct faculty. I was underpaid but I had healthcare, not a trivial benefit. I also had a shared office and a supportive department chair—two factors that made the experience more professional and pleasant than that of many adjuncts who work at less progressive colleges.

Thus, I do not wish to complain but to speak on behalf of adjuncts and to lend insight into the intractable nature of this problem. I want to focus on structural aspects of the adjunct system but also the subjective experience of being an adjunct professor. I do this because humans are thinking, talking, interpreting creatures with rich inner lives. To understand an industry, or broader economic changes, it is not enough to consider these in aggregate. If we really want to understand how our country is changing—how, for instance, our universities are evolving or how our towns are changing as literally millions of factory jobs have been lost, we need to attend to how it *feels* to be a person in each of these situations. I use testimony, then, to capture a mood, a feeling, and in doing so to hopefully shed light on American politics in the 21st century.

I want to begin by discussing what I and many others call the "adjunct trap." A PhD is a highly specialized degree, it takes years of dedication and hard work but it does not usually develop broadly transferable skills. Once the degree is completed there is often considerable disappointment as one finds that the only academic jobs available are insecure, poorly paid adjunct positions and the degree holder is not well qualified to do anything else. (The prospects for a good job of course vary by discipline). This is especially true in the humanities and social sciences, where many of the skills one develops are not highly valued in the broader labor market. Careful reading, thoughtful and clear writing, rigorous thinking and the ability to develop and assess arguments are undervalued skills, even in the labor market for the professional classes. Thus, we fall into the adjunct trap in part because there is no obvious exit path. And the thought of returning to school, to obtain a more practical degree, is a deeply un-appealing thought after having just spent 6 or 7 years completing a doctorate.

What does it feel like to be in the adjunct trap? To be an adjunct professor is to be low-income, per-haps in debt, having paid the opportunity cost of lost income for 5, 6, maybe 7 or more years while working on the degree. New PhDs need immediate income. Adjunct work, particularly if one teaches a large number of classes, promises just such in-come. Not a lot, but enough to pay rent. They then teach and continue to apply to better jobs. This is the fate of many new and not so new PhDs. Bad pay, endless teaching, and endless job applications in your spare time, not to mention the experience of being a second class citizen in the hierarchy of academia. It is exceedingly difficult, in such a situ-ation, to find the time or the energy to retrain or pursue a new career path full-heartedly. This is the adjunct trap.

So why do they do it? One reason, which is the same for teachers everywhere, is that teaching is really important. It is a fundamental component of a democratic society and it is deeply rewarding much of the time. Many people will teach, even for low pay, on the basis of this motivation. Another reason, however, is more sinister.

The academic system is in an important sense fraudulent. Every year thousands of ambitious, motivated, smart students begin PhD programs. Their labor as teaching assistants (TAs) makes the university run. Indeed, the modern research university genuinely could not function without thousands of graduate students working as TAs who do all the grading, answer student emails, teach discussion sections and exam reviews, and generally act as an intermediary between the students and the professors. It is not an exaggeration to say that most large universities would instantly cease to function without their TAs. They play a key part in making the undergraduate educational experience a good one. TAs, unlike some professors at research schools, actually know the students by name, read, grade, and comment on their work, and build mentoring relationships with them. In addition, the modern research machine would not function without a large number of graduate students working as research assistants for professors on various projects.

Why is this fraudulent? Because the graduate students, who are not well-compensated for their labor, are under the impression that their years of hard work will result in a job similar to those held by the tenured faculty that they work with. This is in many cases a lie. Very few graduate students will ever end up as tenured professors at research universities. Rather, if they are lucky, they will find their way into a job at a teaching university with the possibility of tenure. The remainder will serve in adjunct and other non-tenured faculty positions. The point can be rephrased as a rhetorical question: how many graduate students would make the effort to earn a PhD if they knew that the result of their doctorate would be an adjunct position?

The responsibility for this situation lies largely with university administrators, not faculty. In fact, many tenured faculty are sensitive to the plight of adjuncts and involved in organizing on this issue. (The faculty I worked with, both as a graduate student and as an adjunct professor, were deeply sympathetic to the challenges facing young scholars and adjunct professors). The problem, as others have diagnosed, is that research universities today are effectively run by a large, managerial class of administrators who want to market the university brand to potential students and to keep labor costs low. Does this matter beyond the academy? Yes, for many reasons, one of which is that America's most prestigious universities produce a largely self-enclosed class of intellectual elites while also educating the undergraduate elites who will go on to work in Wall Street, Silicon Valley, and other dominant realms of the American economy.

This personal testimony would not be complete without a focus on the questions of meaning, identity, and purpose, and it is here that I connect my experience to the broader experiences of other American workers. To invest years of one's life in a doctorate (or any career path) is to cultivate an intense love for the object of one's study and the industry (in this case, the academic world) in which one is housed. This provides, at its best, a sense of place, purpose, and dignity. One of the answers for why so many work as adjuncts and cling to the hope of a better job coming along is because this is who they are—they have built a life and an identity as a scholar. To abdicate would be a painful, wrenching process. Who would willingly cast themselves adrift, leaving behind both their income and their sense of place in the world?

This is precisely what has been forced onto millions of Americans and the hardest hit have been those with the least income, family wealth, and education. Given this, it is no surprise that so many Americans are dying the "deaths of despair" from suicide, drug abuse, and alcoholism.

Broadening the Scope: The High School and College Compacts

Without suggesting that the life of an academic is the same as that of a manual laborer or an indebted undergrad, we can draw some lessons here that have broader applicability. The pain of America's heartland as its factories close, its downtowns crumble, and its civic culture continues to fray is almost impossible to put into words. It too is a loss of dignity, purpose, and a sense of possessing an important place in this country and the world. This is an experience that America's political and economic elites almost by definition cannot know. The subjective aspect of job loss is as important as the lost money, and is manifest in divorce, drug and alcohol abuse, and suicide. There is a reason these deaths are increasing among poor and working class Americans. *They are justified in their despair.*

Those, however, who can speak to this pain have found a resonance with American voters that initially surprised almost everyone. Both Bernie Sanders and Donald Trump, in different ways, have tapped into this searing pain that results from the loss of a secure income and a secure identity. This pain, in my own experience, can tend in two directions—either a sense of loss and disillusion, which leads to apathy and despair, or a sense of rage at those responsible, which can be empowering. If the Sanders campaign directs this rage at the financial elites that deserve so much blame for the current economic predicament, the Trump campaign directed (and directs) much of this pain towards Republican Party insiders (who deserve blame) as well as powerless outsiders—immigrants, refugees, minorities (who are not responsible for the structural problems facing the economy).

As William Greider puts it, Sanders represents the "high road" to the future and Trump the "low road." Sanders connects to a feeling that is widely shared among American undergraduates and recent college graduates, who, after attaining what they thought was a ticket to the upper-middle class, find themselves in debt and without good job prospects. This is the violation of the college compact. It is not hard to see why he is so popular among young people. At its best, the 2016 and 2020 Sanders campaigns speak to participants in all three compacts all across the country —unemployed or underemployed and underpaid workers in America's heartland, indebted college students, and lower-level professional class workers increasingly stuck in precarious positions. To repeat, this is what happens when income gains and power are concentrated at the top. When living standards decline for a majority (over a span of decades) while skyrocketing for a tiny elite, it is clear that some shared sense of how America is to be organized has broken down, unravelled, or just been completely cast aside.

I am suggesting that there is an instructive parallel between the experience of adjunct faculty (experiencing the collapse of the graduate school compact) undergrads (experiencing the collapse of the college compact), and that of those employed in the disappearing manufacturing sector or doing other difficult manual work (experiencing the more severe collapse of the high school compact). This experience includes for all three groups a sense of working hard and playing by the rules, with the hope and expectation that this will result in a career that includes good pay, security, and a sense of dignity and pride in one's work. When this pact is broken, the result is shattering. One of the subjective responses is to experience a profound sense of having been treated unfairly.[126]

In the case of the loss of factory jobs in America, we lack the public language to even express what is happening. The phrase "left behind" is often employed, as in "America's heartland is being left behind." This is a euphemism for what is happening, nothing more. The correct word to describe what happens to a town when its key industries leave is "destroyed." As in, "much of America's heartland has effectively been destroyed by the loss of millions of manufacturing jobs." This is the consequence of the unraveling of the high school compact. Thinking in terms of a compact, and a set of rules that one must play by in return for a secure living, helps to uncover what is so infuriating to those on the losing end of the broken compact. They aren't just struggling financially—they have been treated unfairly. They have been, in a word, wronged.

We need to recognize how broken the promise of the American dream is when many Americans, from college professors to factory workers, are experiencing declining standards of living. To be clear, this lament is hardly contained to white Americans. Many working class Americans are not white and the great recession, among other things, wiped out much of the middle class wealth that had accumulated among black families over the past few decades. This condition applies, in varying ways, to Americans of all colors who are not at the very heights of the income and wealth ladder.

This is important because what I am describing is not limited to America's universities. As Trish Kahle notes writing for *Jacobin*, "casualization of the labor force in higher education — the rise of the adjunct tier of the professoriate — and enormous increases in administrative hires mirror changes in employment in other industries." With the unraveling of the college compact, a bachelor's degree is not the ticket to an upper-middle class life that it used to be—increasingly, a master's or doctorate is recommended, perhaps even required. And as I have discussed, even a doctorate is no guarantee of a middle-class income. "Middle-class workers, *without elite degrees*, face discrimination all across a labor market that increasingly privileges elaborate education and extravagant training."[127] Furthermore, we should expect and indeed want creative, ambitious students to be interested in a life of research and teaching. It would be a terrible outcome to see many of our brightest students turn away from an academic career because of the adjunctification of America's universities.

In response to the tumult of the 1960s, political theorists Sheldon Wolin and John Schaar made the following observation, as relevant now as it was decades ago: There are an "increasing number of young people who are being educated and encouraged to unsatisfiable expectations about their adult roles. A superfluous population is being produced, one that cannot simultaneously be absorbed and fulfilled. Moreover, education is designed to increase dissatisfactions. It encourages self-consciousness and critical awareness, and nourishes hope of a better life where beauty and dignity are possible. As yet, technological society has not figured out how to cope with its superfluous human beings."[128]

It is common to conclude with some proposed solutions for how to deal with these problems.

The first step to solving these problems is to develop a shared, public language that allows us to talk about them in a clear and compelling manner. Doing so will enable a movement to achieve more success in the future, in making college more affordable, curbing administrative bloat, expanding access to health care, strengthening unions in all industries, and transforming adjunct positions into tenured ones. It is my contention that until we understand intuitively what it feels like to be an adjunct professor, a displaced factory worker, a student trapped in debt, we will not be able to win at the ballot box and we will not be able to overturn elite rule. Hopefully this marks one small step toward improving our understanding and thus making this agenda more achievable, now and in the future.

CHAPTER SEVEN: REFERENCES AND NOTES

Acknowledgments

Thanks, as always, to my parents for their support and careful reading of the manuscript. Thanks as well to my sister for her continued enthusiasm and support regarding my intellectual endeavors. An artist, she understands that some dreams have to be chased, regardless of whether they will ever be caught. Thanks to Alyssa for love and encouragement and to friends who have been interested in and supportive of my past work.

Select Bibliography

Abramowitz, Alan. *The Great Alignment: Race, Party Transformation, and the Rise of Donald Trump*. New Haven: Yale University Press, 2018.

Achen, Christopher H. and Larry M. Bartels. *Democracy for Realists: Why Elections Do Not Produce*

Responsive Government. Princeton: Princeton University Press, 2017.

Anderson, Elizabeth. *Private Government: How Employers Rule Our Lives (and Why We Don't Talk About It)*. Princeton: Princeton University Press, 2017.

Bacevich, Andrew. *The Age of Illusions: How America Squandered Its Cold War Victory*. New York: Metropolitan Books, 2020.

Baiocchi, Gianpaolo and Ernesto Ganuza. *Popular Democracy: The Paradox of Participation*. Stanford: Stanford University Press, 2017.

Baker, Dean. *Rigged: How Globalization and the Rules of the Modern Economy Were Structured to Make the Rich Richer.* Washington, DC: Center for Economic and Policy Research, 2016.

Barber, Benjamin R. *Strong Democracy: Participatory Politics for a New Age.* Berkeley: University of California Press, 1984.

Barber, Benjamin R. *The Conquest of Politics: Liberal Philosophy in Democratic Times*. Princeton: Princeton University Press, 1988.

Bartels, Larry M. *Unequal Democracy: The Political Economy of the New Gilded Age.* Princeton: Princeton University Press, 2008.

Beaubien, Jason. "There's a New Kind of Inequality. And It's Not About Income." *NPR.* December 9,

2019.

Blanchflower, David G. *Not Working: Where Have All the Good Jobs Gone?* Princeton: Princeton University Press, 2019.

Boyte, Harry C. *Awakening Democracy Through Public Work: Pedagogies of Empowerment.* Nashville: Vanderbilt University Press, 2018.

Boyte, Harry C. *Community is Possible.* New York: Harper & Row Publishers, 1984.

Brennan, Jason. *Against Democracy.* Princeton: Princeton University Press, 2016.

Brennan, Jason and Phillip Magness. *Cracks in the Ivory Tower: The Moral Mess of Higher Education.* New York: Oxford University Press, 2019.

Brown, Wendy. *In the Ruins of Neoliberalism: The Rise of Antidemocratic Politics in the West.* New York: Columbia University Press, 2019.

Brown, Wendy. *Undoing the Demos: Neoliberalism's Stealth Revolution.* New York: Zone Books, 2015.

Caplan, Bryan. *The Myth of the Rational Voter: Why Democracies Choose Bad Policies.* Princeton: Princeton University Press, 2007.

Carey, Kevin. "The Bleak Job Landscape of Adjunctopia for PhDs," *New York Times.* March 6, 2020. https://www.nytimes.com/2020/03/05/upshot/academic-job-crisis-phd.html.

Casselman, Ben. "Stop Saying Trump's Win Had Nothing to do with Economics," *fivethirtyeight*, January 9, 2017. https://fivethirtyeight.com/features/stop-saying-trumps-win-had-nothing-to-do-with-economics/

Childress, Herb. *The Adjunct Underclass: How America's Colleges Betrayed Their Faculty, Their Students, and Their Mission*. Chicago: The University of Chicago Press, 2019.

Chomsky, Noam. *American Power and the New Mandarins*. New York: Pantheon Books, 1969.

Chomsky, Noam. *On Anarchism*. New York: Penguin Books, 2013.

Chomsky, Noam. *Internationalism or Extinction*. New York: Routledge, 2020.

Coates, Ta-Nehisi. *We Were Eight Years in Power: An American Tragedy*. New York: One World, 2018.

Cohen, G.A. *If You're An Egalitarian How Come You're So Rich?* Cambridge: Harvard University Press, 2000.

Coles, Romand. *Visionary Pragmatism: Radical and Ecological Democracy in Neoliberal Times.* Durham: Duke University Press, 2016.

Connolly, William E. *Aspirational Fascism: The Struggle for Multifaceted Democracy under Trumpism*. Minneapolis: University of Minnesota Press,

2017.

Connolly, William E. *Climate Machines, Fascist Drives, and Truth*. Durham: Duke University Press, 2019.

Connolly, William E. *The Fragility of Things: Self-Organizing Processes, Neoliberal Fantasies, and Democratic Activism*. Durham: Duke University Press, 2013.

Cramer, Katherine J. *The Politics of Resentment: Rural Consciousness in Wisconsin and the Rise of Scott Walker*. Chicago: The University of Chicago Press, 2016.

Crouch, Colin. *The Strange Non-Death of Neoliberalism*. Malden, MA: Polity Press, 2011.

Deresiewicz, William. *Excellent Sheep: The Miseducation of American Elite and the Way to a Meaningful Life*. New York: Free Press, 2014.

Desmond, Matthew. *Evicted: Poverty and Profit in the American City*. New York: Crown Publishers, 2016.

Dietze, Pia, Ana Gantman, H. Hannah Nam, and Laura Niemi. "Marginalized ideas are key to scientific progress" October 10, 2019, *Nature Human Behavior 3 (1024), 2019.*

Donoghue, Frank. *The Last Professors: The Corporate University and the Fate of the Humanities*. New

York: Fordham University Press, 2008.

Domhoff, G. William. *Who Rules America? Challenges to Corporate and Class Dominance. Sixth Edition.* New York: McGraw-Hill, 2010.

Drezner, Daniel W. *The Ideas Industry: How Pessimists, Partisans, and Plutocrats are Transforming the Marketplace of Ideas.* New York: Oxford University Press, 2017.

Dzur, Albert. *Democracy Inside: Participatory Innovations in Unlikely Places.* New York: Oxford University Press, 2019.

Dzur, Albert W. *Rebuilding Public Institutions Together: Professionals and Citizens in a Participatory Democracy.* Ithaca: Cornell University Press, 2018.

Frank, Robert. *Falling Behind: How Inequality Harms the Middle Class.* Berkeley: University of California Press, 2007.

Frank, Thomas. *Listen, Liberal, or What Ever Happened to the Party of the People?* New York: Picador, 2016.

Frankfurt, Harry G. *On Inequality.* Princeton: Princeton University Press, 2015.

Fraser, Nancy. *The Old is Dying and the New Cannot Be Born: From Progressive Neoliberalism to Trump and Beyond.* New York: Verso Books, 2019.

Freire, Paulo. *Pedagogy of the Oppressed.* New York:

Penguin Books, 1996.

Frost, Amber A'Lee. "The WeWork Con," *Jacobin*, 11/252019.

Gilens, Martin. *Affluence and Influence: Economic Inequality and Political Power in America.* Princeton: Princeton University Press, 2012.

Gilens, Martin and Benjamin Page. *Democracy in America? What Has Gone Wrong and What We Can Do About It.* Chicago: The University of Chicago Press, 2017.

Gilens, Martin and Benjamin Page. "Testing Theories of American Politics: Elites, Interest Groups, and Average Citizens." *Perspectives on Politics* 12, no. 3 (2014).

Gilman, Hollie Russon. *Democracy Reinvented: Participatory Budgeting and Civic Innovation in America.* Washington, DC: Brookings Institute Press, 2016.

Ginsberg, Benjamin. *The Fall of the Faculty*. New York: Oxford University Press, 2011.

Goldstein, Amy. *Janesville: An American Story*. New York: Simon and Schuster, 2017.

Graeber, David. *Bullshit Jobs: A Theory*. New York: Simon and Schuster, 2018.

Harvey, David. *A Brief History of Neoliberalism.* New York: Oxford University Press, 2005.

Hayes, Chris. *Twilight of the Elites: America After Meritocracy*. New York: Broadway, 2012.

Hedges, Chris. *America: The Farewell Tour*. New York: Simon and Schuster, 2018.

Hedges, Chris. *Death of the Liberal Class*. New York: Nation Books, 2010.

Hetherington, Marc and Jonathan Weiler. *Prius or Pickup? How the Answers to Four Simple Questions Explain America's Great Divide*. New York: Houghton Mifflin Harcourt, 2018.

Hobbs-Morgan, Chase M. *Greenhouse Democracy: A Political Theory for Climate Change.* Dissertation: University of Minnesota, 2017.

Hochschild, Arlie Russell. *Strangers in Their Own Land: Anger and Mourning on the American Right.* New York: The New Press, 2016.

Hoffower, Hillary. "The Typical US Worker Can No Longer Afford a Family on a Year's Salary, Showing the Dire State of America's Middle Class," *Business Insider*, February 25, 2020. https://www.businessinsider.com/america-middle-class-living-expenses-family-of-four-2020-2?fbclid=IwAR1RtLwB4KlgYNhy5TB5nr5gtef-sXJ9qIUI9ZUneW5ch3z-0lxZojUeVeBY.

Irwin, Douglas A. *Free Trade Under Fire.* Princeton: Princeton University Press, 2002.

Klein, Naomi. *The Shock Doctrine: The Rise of Disaster Capitalism*. New York: Picador, 2007.

Kelly, Kim. "Strangled by a Safety Net", *The Baffler* No. 47, September 2019.

Kolodny, Niko. "Democracy for Idealists." Available at https://www.ocf.berkeley.edu/~ngkolodny//DemocracyForIdealist2.pdf?fbclid=IwAR3_xFZ47MzPL0i0qNDDbkBOT-d1ST5sMNEsID1j3lQ6qBQAKt3yH9E6sPTs

Krugman, Paul. *The Conscience of a Liberal*. New York: W.W. Norton and Company, 2007.
Leonhardt, David. "How Centrist Bias Hurts Sanders and Warren," New York Times, December 22, 2019.

Lerner, Josh. *Everyone Counts: Could "Participatory Budgeting" Change Democracy?* Ithaca: Cornell University Press, 2014.

Lerner, Josh. *Making Democracy Fun: How Game Design Can Empower Citizens and Transform Politics.* Cambridge, MA: MIT Press, 2014.

Lopez, Ian Haney. *Merge Left: Fusing Race and Class, Winning Elections, and Saving America.* New York: The New Press, 2019.

Malleson, Tom. *After Occupy: Economic Democracy for the 21st Century*. New York: Oxford University Press, 2014.

Malleson, Tom. *Fired Up About Capitalism*. Toronto: Between the Lines, 2016.

Markovits, Daniel. *The Meritocracy Trap: How America's Foundational Myth Feeds Inequality, Dismantles the Middle Class, and Devours the Elite*. New York: Penguin Press, 2019.

Miller, James. *Can Democracy Work? A Short History of a Radical Idea, from Ancient Athens to Our World*. New York: Farrar, Straus, and Giroux, 2018.

Mills, C. Wright. *The Power Elite*. New York: Oxford University Press, 1956.

Mouffe, Chantal. *For a Left Populism*. New York: Verso Books, 2018.

Mouffe, Chantal. *On the Political*. New York: Routledge, 2005.

Nichols, John. "Bernie Sanders Won't Play Your Game", *The Nation.* January 15, 2020. https://www.thenation.com/article/bernie-sanders-trade-climate/.

Noah, Timothy. *The Great Divergence: America's Growing Inequality Crisis and What We Can Do About It*. New York: Bloomsbury Press, 2012.

Norris, Pippa and Ronald Inglehart. *Cultural Backlash: Trump, Brexit, and Authoritarian Populism*. New York: Cambridge University Press, 2019.

Olson, Randy. *Houston, We Have a Narrative: Why Science Needs Story.* Chicago: The University of Chicago Press, 2015.

Packer, George. *The Unwinding: An Inner History of the New America.* New York: Farrar, Straus, and Giroux, 2013.

Pateman, Carole. *Participation and Democratic Theory.* New York: Cambridge University Press, 1970.

Pateman, Carole. "Participatory Democracy Revisited," *Perspectives on Politics* 10, no. 1 (2012) : 7-19.

Payne, Keith. *The Broken Ladder: How Inequality Affects the Way We Think, Live, and Die.* New York: Penguin Books, 2017.

Peck, Jamie. *Constructions of Neoliberal Reason.* New York: Oxford University Press, 2010.

Piketty, Thomas. *Capital and Ideology.* Cambridge, MA: Harvard University Press, 2020.

Piketty, Thomas. *Capital in the 21st Century.* Cambridge, MA: Harvard University Press, 2014.

Piketty, Thomas. *Why Save the Bankers?* New York: Houghton Mifflin Harcourt, 2016.

Przeworski, Adam. *Why Bother With Elections?* Medford, MA: Polity Press, 2018.

Putnam, Robert. Our Kids: *The American Dream in*

Crisis. New York: Simon and Schuster, 2015.

Rancière, Jacques. *The Ignorant Schoolmaster: Five Lessons in Intellectual Emancipation*. Palo Alto: Stanford University Press, 1991.

Rawls, John. *A Theory of Justice*. Cambridge, MA: Harvard University Press, 1971.

Reich, Robert B. *Aftershock: The Next Economy and America's Future*. New York: Vintage Books, 2011.

Reich, Robert B. *Saving Capitalism: For the Many, Not the Few*. New York: Vintage Books, 2016.

Reich, Robert B. *The System: Who Rigged It, How We Fix It*. New York: Knopf, 2020.

Reiter, Bern. *The Crisis of Liberal Democracy and the Path Ahead: Alternatives to Political Representation and Capitalism*. New York: Rowman & Littlefield, 2017.

Rodriguez, Francisco and Dani Rodrik. "Trade Policy and Economic Growth: A Skeptic's Guide to the Cross-National Evidence." *BER/Macroeconomics Annual*, vol 15(1), pages 261-325.

Ross, Martha and Nicole Bateman, "Low unemployment isn't worth much if the jobs barely pay." *Brookings*, January 8, 2020. https://www.brookings.edu/blog/the-avenue/2020/01/08/low-unemployment-isnt-worth-much-if-the-jobs-barely-pay/?

fbclid=IwAR3zdCd8dEeyQS_FyJ7nLtcgTlud-gRQA5_yIG0FqkaaIqyFKx-3NtWbG8fc.

Rothwell, Jonathan. *A Republic of Equals: A Manifesto for a Just Society.* Princeton: Princeton University Press, 2019.

Rousseau, Jean-Jacques. *The Basic Political Writings*. Indianapolis: Hackett Publishing Company, 2011.

Saez, Emmanuel and Gabriel Zucman. *The Triumph of Injustice: How the Rich Dodge Taxes and How to Make Them Pay.* New York: W.W. Norton & Company, 2019.

Savage, Luke. "Neoliberalism? Never Heard of It?" *Jacobin.* 11/03/2019.

Schumacher, E.F. *Small is Beautiful: Economics as if People Mattered.* New York: Harper Perennial, 1975/2010.

Schumpeter, Joseph. *Capitalism, Socialism, and Democracy*: Third Edition. New York: Harper Perennial, 2008.

Smith, Hedrick. *Who Stole the American Dream?* New York: Random House, 2012.

Smith, Marcie. "Don't Let Liberals Write Off Workers in "Flyover Country," *Jacobin.* December 17, 2019.

Srnicek, Nick and Alex Williams. *Inventing the Future: Postcapitalism and a World Without Work.* New

York: Verso Books, 2015.

Standing, Guy. *The Precariat: The New Dangerous Class*. New York: Bloomsbury, 2011.

Standing, Guy. *A Precariat Charter: From Denizens to Citizens*. New York: Bloomsbury, 2014.

Stein, Samuel. *Capital City: Gentrification and the Real Estate State*. New York: Verso Books, 2019.

Stiglitz, Joseph E. *Globalization and Its Discontents Revisited: Anti-Globalization in the Era of Trump.* New York: W.W. Norton and Company, 2018.

Stiglitz, Joseph E. *People, Power, and Profits: Progressive Capitalism for an Age of Discontent.* New York: W.W. Norton and Company, 2019.

Stiglitz, Joseph E. *The Great Divide: Unequal Societies and What We Can Do About Them*. New York: W.W. Norton and Company, 2015.

Stizlitz, Joseph E. *The Price of Inequality: How Today's Divided Society Endangers Our Future*. New York: W.W. Norton and Company, 2013.

Stoller, Matt. "The Question is Whether We Live in a Democracy or a Corporate State," *ProMarket.* January 2, 2020. https://promarket.org/the-question-is-whether-we-live-in-a-democracy-or-a-corporate-state/

Taylor, Astra. *Democracy May Not Exist But We'll Miss It When It's Gone*. New York: Metropolitan

Books, 2019.

Vick, Jason. *A 21st Century Defense of Participatory Democracy*. Dissertation: University of California, Irvine. 2016.

Vick, Jason. *Does Democracy Have a Future?* Independent. 2019.

Vick, Jason. "Participatory vs. Radical Democracy in the 21st Century: Carole Pateman, Jacques Rancière, and Sheldon Wolin." *New Political Science*; 37, No. 2, (2015), 204-223.

Weisbrot, Mark. *Failed: What the "Experts" Got Wrong About the Global Economy*. New York: Oxford University Press, 2015.

Winters, Jeffrey A. *Oligarchy*. New York: Cambridge University Press, 2011.

Wolin, Sheldon S. *Democracy Incorporated: Managed Democracy and the Specter of Inverted Totalitarianism*. Princeton: Princeton University Press, 2008.

Wolin, Sheldon S. *Fugitive Democracy and Other Essays*. Princeton: Princeton University Press, 2016.

Wolin, Sheldon S. *The Presence of the Past*. Baltimore: The Johns Hopkins University Press, 1989.

Wolin, Sheldon S. And John H. Schaar. *The Berkeley Rebellion and Beyond: Essays on Politics and Education in the Technological Society*. New York: Vintage, 1970.

Zinn, Howard. "The Problem is Civil Obedience," *History Is A Weapon*, November 1970. Available at https://www.historyisaweapon.com/defcon1/zinnproblemobedience.html.

[1] Sheldon Wolin, *The Presence of the Past* (Baltimore: The Johns Hopkins University Press, 1989), p. 5.

[2] Sheldon Wolin, *The Presence of the Past* (Baltimore: The Johns Hopkins University Press, 1989), p. 8.

[3] Claims by Christopher Achen and Larry Bartels at the end of *Democracy for Realists* that it would be good for the poor to have more political influence ring hollow after spending the entire text critiquing the knowledge and competence of the citizenry and opposing progressive efforts, both past and present, to expand citizen access and participation. How else, exactly, are the poor to have more political influence, if not through *increased* participation in politics?

[4] Joseph Schumpeter, *Capitalism, Socialism, and Democracy: Third Edition* (New York: Harper Perennial, 2008).

[5] Sheldon S. Wolin, *The Presence of the Past* (Baltimore: The Johns Hopkins University Press, 1989), p.

[6] For an extended discussion of this point, see Sheldon S. Wolin, *The Presence of the Past* (Baltimore: The Johns Hopkins University Press, 1989), particularly chapter five.

[7] For more on this point, see Benjamin R. Barber, *Strong Democracy: Participatory Politics for a New Age* (Berkeley: University of California Press, 1984) and *The Conquest of Politics: Liberal Philosophy in Democratic Times* (Princeton: Princeton University Press, 1988).

[8] Sheldon S. Wolin, The Presence of the Past (Baltimore: The Johns Hopkins University Press, 1989), p. 191.

[9] Sheldon S. Wolin, *The Presence of the Past* (Baltimore: The Johns Hopkins University Press, 1989), pp. 191, 81.

[10] For a representative work that is generally in favor of free trade and the global trade regime, see Douglas A. Irwin, *Free*

Trade Under Fire (Princeton: Princeton University Press, 2002). In this book Irwin critiques a number of challenges to free trade.

[11] See, for instance, Wendy Brown, *Undoing the Demos* and *In the Ruins of Neoliberalism*; David Harvey, *A Brief History of Neoliberalism*; Jamie Peck, *Constructions of Neoliberal Reason*; William Connolly, *The Fragility of Things*. Though he doesn't use the term, see also Sheldon Wolin's powerful account of the merging of corporate and political power in *Democracy Incorporated*.

[12] Luke Savage, "Neoliberalism? Never Heard of It?" *Jacobin* 11/03/2019

[13] It is important to recognize that those who are harmed tend to be citizens at the median or lower income level. In other words, the current global trade regime harms not elites but middle and working class citizens. This point will be stressed throughout.

[14] Confirming Chomsky's point, economists Emmanuel Saez and Gabriel Zucman observe in passing that "what most free trade agreements are these days" are efforts to "protect the property rights of investors." See *The Triumph of Injustice*, p.126. Chomsky also rightly observes that global trade doesn't have to be this way. We suffer from a form of "globalization that has been designed in the interests of the investor class and transnational capital," from *Internationalism or Extinction* (New York: Routledge, 2020), p. 82.

[15] Daniel Markovits provides some evidence that the absolute living standards for the poorest of the poor in the US have increased since the 1960s. While this may be true, it doesn't invalidate my broader thesis: the majority of working and middle class Americans have seen their relative and absolute living standards decline as they have been pushed down towards the poor. The middle class really has evaporated as the richest of the rich have taken off. For compelling evidence that life has stayed the same or worsened for the very poorest Americans (in absolute and relative terms), see Matthew Desmond's excellent *Evicted: Poverty and Profit in the American City* (New York: Crown Publishers, 2016). I per-

sonally find Desmond's case studies and qualitative analysis to be more convincing.

[16] John Nichols, "Bernie Sanders Won't Play Your Game", *The Nation*, January 15, 2020. https://www.thenation.com/article/bernie-sanders-trade-climate/.

[17] This average masks the fact that work hours vary for different classes of citizens. Roughly the top half of the income distribution work more hours while some of the bottom half actually work fewer hours than in the 1970s. This is not a triumph, however. The working poor struggle with under-employment because they are paid hourly wages and need *more hours* just to pay their bills. While many Americans are overworked, a substantial number of working poor struggle with low-pay *and* low-hours. See Daniel Markovits, *The Meritocracy Trap* and David Blanchflower, *Not Working*.

[18] Matthew Desmond powerfully documents the central role eviction plays in the lives of the poor, noting that "every year in [the USA] people are evicted from their homes not by the tens of thousands or even the hundreds of thousands but by the millions." See *Evicted: Poverty and Profit in the American City* (New York: Crown Publishers, 2016), p. 295.

[19] A report from the Manhattan Institute notes that "college tuition has more than doubled since the 1970s" and cumulative student loan debt is currently $1.5 trillion (as of 2020). In addition, relating to point 4, housing costs have increased by nearly 40% since the 1970s and healthcare generally costs thousands more dollars per year. See the summary in Hillary Hoffower, "The Typical US Worker Can No Longer Afford a Family on a Year's Salary, Showing the Dire State of America's Middle Class," *Business Insider*, February 25, 2020.

[20] As Emmanuel Saez and Gabriel Zucman note, the only other recent example of life expectancy declining during peacetime occurred in Russia in the 1990s amidst the economic chaos that resulted from the transition to oligarchic capitalism.

[21] See Blanchflower, *Not Working: Where Have All the Good Jobs Gone?* (Princeton: Princeton University Press, 2019), p. 61.

[22] David Blanchflower in *Not Working: Where Have All the Good Jobs Gone?* notes that in addition to the opioid epidemic and other deaths of despair, suicide rates in the USA are at their highest since 1999. In his book *The Age of Illusions* (New York: Metropolitan Books, 2020), Andrew Bacevich offers a somewhat similar list of problems plaguing contemporary America. While there is overlap, my list is more focused on the economy and the related impacts of economic decline. I generally agree with Bacevich that many of the factors he discusses "suggest a society in which discontent, disfunction, and sheer perversity [are] rampant." See *The Age of Illusions*, pp. 146-149.

[23] Something on the order of 8 million manufacturing jobs have been lost in recent decades. Markovits mentions one study that estimates the USA would need to create *25 million* good manufacturing jobs to recreate the labor economy and middle class of the 1960s and 1970s.

[24] Robert Frank in his book *Falling Behind* discusses evidence for increased work hours, increased commutes, less sleep, and more income spent on housing. According to his data the average American man works 100 hours more per year than in the 1970s and the average American woman works 200 more hours per year. See also the data summarized in Hillary Hoffower, "The Typical US Worker Can No Longer Afford a Family on a Year's Salary, Showing the Dire State of America's Middle Class," *Business Insider*, February 25, 2020.

[25] Rothwell makes a compelling case in this regard, though his claim that trade is not also a major contributing factor to US inequality is less compelling. The global trade regime of recent decades is almost certainly a key factor in the massive loss of unionized, middle-class manufacturing jobs in America. For more see his *A Republic of Equals.*

[26] Unfortunately, even countries with higher rates of unionization and more friendly labor laws have still felt the unequalizing pinch of the global trade regime. As Daniel Drezner notes, the gini coefficient, which measures inequality, "increased in 80% of the advanced industrial economies" between 1980 and 2005. See Daniel W. Drezner, *The Ideas In-*

dustry (New York: Oxford University Press, 2017), p. 62.

[27] Many European countries have also seen declines in unionization rates but they are generally starting from much higher rates and have seen smaller reductions.

[28] See Timothy Noah, *The Great Divergence*, for an excellent review of inequality literature that attempts to identify how much various factors, from declining unionization to increased trade, have impacted inequality in the USA.

[29] This is, in part, and empirical question, though it may be difficult to answer with precision. Note, however, that it is conceptually possible that global trade, as it has been practiced, has destroyed more good jobs in the US than it has created. There is nothing absurd in this hypothesis.

[30] Markovits, in the final chapter of *The Meritocracy Trap* provides helpful suggestions for how the US economy might shift back towards creating more mid-skilled, middle-class jobs.

[31] See Martha Ross and Nicole Bateman, "Low unemployment isn't worth much if the jobs barely pay," *Brookings*, January 8, 2020. https://www.brookings.edu/blog/the-avenue/2020/01/08/low-unemployment-isnt-worth-much-if-the-jobs-barely-pay/?fbclid=IwAR3zdCd8dEeyQS_FyJ7nLtcgTludgRQA5_yIG0Fq-kaaIqyFKx-3NtWbG8fc

[32] Hedrick Smith, *Who Stole the American Dream?* (New York: Random House, 2012).

[33] Emmanuel Saez and Gabriel Zucman, *The Triumph of Injustice*, p. 6.

[34] David Blanchflower, *Not Working: Where Have All the Good Jobs Gone?* (Princeton: Princeton University Press, 2019), p. 56.

[35] E.F. Schumacher, *Small is Beautiful: Economics as if People Mattered* (New York: Harper Perennial), 1975/2010.

[36] Sheldon Wolin, *The Presence of the Past*, pp. 44-45.

[37] Those on the right today seem to have largely forgotten this point, though wise thinkers like Ross Douthat retain an awareness. For more on this point, Katherine Cramer's *The Politics of Resentment* offers a wise, empathetic analysis of

rural identity in Wisconsin and how it is connected to a feeling of decline. Arlie Hochschild's *Strangers in Their Own Land* and Amy Goldstein's *Janesville: An American Story* also offer powerful depictions of those battered by decades of economic and community decline. Combined with George Packer's *The Unwinding*, these books offer a powerful, troubling set of qualitative insights into these economic, cultural, and political trends.

[38] Chris Hedges, *America: The Farewell Tour*, p. 41

[39] Sheldon S. Wolin, *The Presence of the Past* ,p. 17

[40] Sheldon S. Wolin, *The Presence of the Past*, p. 161.

[41] Daniel Markovits, *The Meritocracy Trap* (New York: Penguin Press, 2019), p. 30.

[42] Harry C. Boyte, *Awakening Democracy Through Public Work: Pedagogies of Empowerment* (Nashville: Vanderbilt University Press, 2018), p. 103.

[43] Adam Przeworski, *Why Bother With Elections?*, p. 99.

[44] For more on this point see my *Does Democracy Have a Future?* (Independent: 2019).

[45] Pippa Norris and Ronald Inglehart, *Cultural Backlash: Trump, Brexit, and Authoritarian Populism* (New York: Cambridge University Press, 2019), p. 158. See the data they present on pp. 158-160.

[46] David Blanchflower, *Not Working: Where Have All the Good Jobs Gone?* (Princeton: Princeton University Press, 2019), p. 74.

[47] David Blanchflower, *Not Working: Where Have All the Good Jobs Gone?* (Princeton: Princeton University Press, 2019, p. 76.

[48] Pippa Norris and Ronald Inglehart, *Cultural Backlash: Trump, Brexit, and Authoritarian Populism* (New York: Cambridge University Press, 2019), p. 161.

[49] In addition to Norris and Inglehart and Blanchflower, see Ben Casselman, "Stop Saying Trump's Win Had Nothing to do with Economics," *fivethirtyeight*, January 9, 2017. https://fivethirtyeight.com/features/stop-saying-trumps-win-had-nothing-to-do-with-economics/. Chapter 10 of Blanchflower's *Not Working* also provides excellent data on the relation between economic stagnation and support

for right-wing populism.

[50] For a detailed discussion of elite policy failure on a wide range of macroeconomic issues, see Mark Weisbrot, *Failed: What the Experts Got Wrong About the Global Economy* (New York: Oxford University Press, 2015).

[51] See Joseph E. Stiglitz, *Globalization and Its Discontents Revisited: Anti-Globalization in the Era of Trump* (W.W. Norton: New York, 2018), for an excellent discussion of the manner in which corporate-led globalization has harmed many workers in both wealthy and poor countries.

[52] Harry G. Frankfurt, *On Inequality* (Princeton: Princeton University Press, 2015), p. 89.

[53] See, for instance, Timothy Noah, *The Great Divergence*; Joseph Stiglitz, *The Price of Inequality* and *The Great Divide*; Paul Krugman, *The Conscience of a Liberal*; Tom Malleson, *After Occupy*; Thomas Piketty, *Capital in the 21st Century*; Robert Putnam, *Our Kids*; Dean Baker, *Rigged*; Robert B. Reich, *Aftershock: The Next Economy and America's Future*; Emmanuel Saez and Gabriel Zucman, *The Triumph of Injustice: How the Rich Dodge Taxes and How to Make Them Pay* (New York: W.W. Norton & Company, 2019).

[54] Emmanuel Saez and Gabriel Zucman put it succinctly: "In 2018, the rich evaded [taxes] more than the working class and middle class due to weak estate tax enforcement, aggressive corporate tax-dodging by multinationals, and offshore individual income tax evasion." From *The Triumph of Injustice: How the Rich Dodge Taxes and How to Make Them Pay* (New York: W.W. Norton & Company, 2019), p. 63.

[55] Emmanuel Saez and Gabriel Zucman, *The Triumph of Injustice: How the Rich Dodge Taxes and How to Make Them Pay* (New York: W.W. Norton & Company, 2019), p 20. See also Jeffrey A. Winters, *Oligarchy* (New York: Cambridge University Press, 2011).

[56] David Blanchfower, *Not Working: Where Have All the Good Jobs Gone?* (Princeton: Princeton University Press, 2019), p. 117. See also Joseph E. Stiglitz, *The Price of Inequality* and *People, Power, and Profits: Progressive Capitalism for an Age of*

Discontent. See also Jason Beaubien, "There's a New Kind of Inequality. And It's Not About Income." *NPR.* December 9, 2019.

[57] See John Rawls, *A Theory of Justice*; G.A. Cohen, *If You're An Egalitarian How Come You're So Rich?*

[58] Keith Payne, *The Broken Ladder: How Inequality Affects the Way We Think, Live, and Die* (New York: Penguin Books, 2017), p. 54.

[59] Keith Payne, *The Broken Ladder: How Inequality Affects the Way We Think, Live, and Die.* (New York: Penguin Books, 2017), p. 195

[60] Jonathan Rothwell, *A Republic of Equals* (Princeton: Princeton University Press, 2019), p. 7.

[61] Keith Payne, *The Broken Ladder: How Inequality Affects the Way We Think, Live, and Die* (New York: Penguin Books, 2017), p. 206.

[62] Adam Przeworski, *Why Bother With Elections?* (Medford, MA: Polity Press, 2018), p. 109

[63] Adam Przeworski, *Why Bother with Elections?* (Medford, MA: Polity Press, 2018), p. 111.

[64] Harry G. Frankfurt, *On Inequality* (Princeton: Princeton University Press, 2015).

[65] Harry G. Frankfurt, *On Inequality* (Princeton: Princeton University Press, 2015) p. 70.

[66] For a detailed, lengthy discussion of "inequality regimes" see Thomas Piketty's magnum opus, *Capital in the 21st Century* and his equally impressive follow-up, *Capital and Ideology.*

[67] Daniel Markovits, *The Meritocracy Trap* (New York: Penguin Press, 2019), p. 29.

[68] Sheldon Wolin, *The Presence of the Past* (Baltimore: The Johns Hopkins University Press, 1989), p. 4.

[69] Sheldon Wolin, *The Presence of the Past* (Baltimore: The Johns Hopkins University Press, 1989), p. 5.

[70] Sheldon Wolin, *The Presence of the Past* (Baltimore: The Johns Hopkins University Press, 1989), p. 58.

[71] I discuss Brennan and the flaws in his thesis in my *Does Democracy Have a Future?*

[72] I discuss some similar questions in *Does Democracy Have a Future?*, particularly in chapters four and five.

[73] Albert W. Dzur, *Democracy Inside: Participatory Innovation in Unlikely Places*, pp. 115.

[74] Lerner quote from Albert W. Dzur, *Democracy Inside: Participatory Innovation in Unlikely Places*, pp. 114. In Lerner's book *Making Democracy Fun: How Game Design Can Empower Citizens and Transform Politics* (Cambridge, MA: MIT Press, 2014) he discusses how insights into game design can be used to create forms of democratic participation that are rewarding and interesting to ordinary citizens.

[75] Noam Chomsky, *On Anarchism* (New York: Penguin Books, 2013), p. 45. See also his *American Power and the New Mandarins* (New York: Pantheon Books, 1969) for extended discussion of the blind spots of intellectuals when discussing the Spanish Civil War, the Vietnam War, and other historical events.

[76] Sheldon Wolin, *The Presence of the Past* (Baltimore: The Johns Hopkins University Press), p. 89. This is also why Jason Brennan's characterization of politically active citizens as "hooligans" who root for their side like a sports team is misguided. Real citizens are not detached experts. We are necessarily invested in the outcomes of political struggles and they are a part of who we are. The idea that we can (or should) treat politics with academic detachment borders on incoherence.

[77] At the end of *Democracy for Realists*, in an abrupt change in focus and tone, the authors state that their criticism of democratic publics also applies to elites before rattling off a couple elite failures. This is deeply unconvincing. They have spent an entire book arguing that the public is ignorant and that this ignorance has direct, negative effects on political outcomes. It is hard to take serious this sudden about-face. Of course there is no inherent contradiction in claiming that both elites and the broader public are ignorant or incom-

petent politically. But there is a contradiction in presenting massive evidence against the expansion of democracy and against greater public involvement and then suddenly saying that elites are bad too. Really? If the public is no worse than elites why can't we expand democracy in all the ways that deliberative and participatory democrats have advocated?

[78] Christopher H. Achen and Larry M. Bartels, *Democracy for Realists: Why Elections Do Not Produce Responsive Government* (Princeton: Princeton University Press, 2016), p. 284.

[79] Christopher H. Achen and Larry M. Bartels, *Democracy for Realists: Why Elections Do Not Produce Responsive Government* (Princeton: Princeton University Press, 2016), p. 325.

[80] Christopher H. Achen and Larry M. Bartels, *Democracy for Realists: Why Elections Do Not Produce Responsive Government* (Princeton: Princeton University Press, 2016), p. 135.

[81] Amber A'Lee Frost, "The WeWork Con," *Jacobin*, 11/252019. We must recognize that criticizing elites is not to unfairly impugn all in positions of power. Some elite (not elitist) professors, like Jacob Hacker and Paul Pierson or Martin Gilens and Benjamin Page, choose to focus more on the problematic power of elites than on the ignorance of the masses. And of course there are the many theorists and commentators I admire and cite throughout my work, some of whom have been affiliated with elite institutions (think Sheldon Wolin, Carole Pateman, Wendy Brown, and Noam Chomsky, to name just a few). But they are going against the grain and to some extent against their class interests when they do so.

[82] Sheldon S. Wolin, "Fugitive Democracy," p. 100, in *Fugitive Democracy and Other Essays* (Princeton: Princeton University Press, 2016). The essays in this collection offer profound, insightful, extended meditations on the nature of the political.

[83] Samuel Stein, *Capital City: Gentrification and the Real Estate State* (New York: Verso Books, 2019).

[84] Christopher H. Achen and Larry M. Bartels, *Democracy for Realists: Why Elections Do Not Produce Responsive Government* (Princeton: Princeton University Press, 2016)p. 92.

[85]Christopher H. Achen and Larry M. Bartels, *Democracy for Realists: Why Elections Do Not Produce Responsive Government* (Princeton: Princeton University Press, 2016), p. 235.

[86] Christopher H. Achen and Larry M. Bartels, *Democracy for Realists: Why Elections Do Not Produce Responsive Government* (Princeton: Princeton University Press, 2016), p. 309.

[87] Katherine Cramer in her book *The Politics of Resentment* (Chicago: The University of Chicago Press, 2016), offers a powerful counter-example to Achen and Bartels. She too is concerned with the role identity plays in shaping our political consciousness, convictions, and behavior. Specifically, Cramer focuses on the role that rural versus urban identities have in impacting politics. The difference, to her credit, is that she does so without resorting to elitist assumptions or arguments. As this book stresses, *of course* identity matters for politics. There is nothing inherently elitist in such a claim; Achen and Bartels *choose* to tie their identity analysis to a broader set of elitist assumptions and arguments.

[88] Emotion is often portrayed as standing in contradiction to reason but the reality is more complicated. Emotion is integral to how humans understand and process the world. It is part of how we acquire knowledge. As Chase M Hobbs-Morgan correctly notes, "If...we know by feeling, to exclude or circumscribe feeling is to exclude knowledge. Perhaps it is unwise to rush into a public sphere overcome with anger; it is at least also unwise to neglect the anger of peoples who have long suffered injustice, or to refuse to attend to one's own angry responses to injustice." See *Greenhouse Democracy: A Political Theory for Climate Change*, p 206

[89] A sarcastic aside: Bartels and Achen present themselves as reluctant but necessary and grand truth-tellers. But there is an *Onion* headline lurking here: "Intellectual elites tell other intellectual elites that non-elites are ignorant and don't deserve power, to universal claim among intellectual elites." I'm inclined to think that epic truth-

telling might be met with more controversy or silence in its early iterations, even if it eventually wins out. A prestigious book deal, major media coverage, academic praise, and so on are not exactly sure signs of a grand new way of thinking.

[90] Katherine J. Cramer, *The Politics of Resentment* (Chicago: The University of Chicago Press, 2016), p. 165.

[91] See the polling data Bryan Caplan discusses in *The Myth of the Rational Voter: Why Democracies Choose Bad Policies* (Princeton: Princeton University Press, 2007). A majority of the public considers layoffs to be negative, whereas a majority of economists see them as positive.

[92] For a discussion of layoffs, see Kim Kelly, "Strangled by a Safety Net", *The Baffler* No. 47, September 2019.

[93] Does this logic apply to other areas of expertise? Arguably not. Getting up and going to work every morning doesn't give me special insight into renaissance literature or theoretical physics. It does, however, give me daily, repeated, qualitative and quantitative information on labor economics, not to mention more subtle, holistic insights and gut intuitions, particularly with regard to precarity, low-pay, stagnant incomes, more work hours, lays offs, plant closures, internal firm hierarchy, authoritarianism, and so forth. Economists may go to work but as a profession they don't experience these more negative aspects. This may be why they are fairly clueless about precarious, low-wage work. For instance, see economist Tyler Cowen's response chapter in Elizabeth Anderson's *Private Government*. Even if we grant every point he makes (which we should not), his remarks at best characterize a subset of good, white collar jobs. *Nothing* he says applies to the majority of American workers, who don't have such jobs. It is therefore not surprising that Anderson, a political scientist and theorist, is more insightful than the economists who authored the response chapters at the end of the book.

[94] For a good discussion of this survey research, see Bryan Caplan, *The Myth of the Rational Voter: Why Democracies Choose Bad Policies* (Princeton: Princeton University Press, 2007), who

firmly sides with the economists in these disputes.

[95] In this insightful interview, Stoller, an idiosyncratic thinker, characterizes elitism in terms similar to my own critique: "What happened from the 1970s onward is that the technocrats, the experts, the people that we were relying on for advice, decided that they shouldn't just be serving democratic ends and offering us advice about what's possible and helping us choose, but that they should, in fact, make those decisions. I think that's where it gets dangerous, with economists essentially making political decisions while hiding the politics in math and models." See "The Question is Whether We Live in a Democracy or a Corporate State," *Pro-Market*, January 2, 2020. https://promarket.org/the-question-is-whether-we-live-in-a-democracy-or-a-corporate-state/

[96] Thomas Piketty, *Capital in the 21st Century* (Cambridge: Harvard University Press, 2014), p. 41.

[97] See Daniel Drezner, *The Ideas Industry* (New York: Oxford University Press, 2017).

[98] Paulo Freire, *Pedagogy of the Oppressed* (New York: Penguin Books, 1996), p. 45.

[99] For more on this point see *Does Democracy Have a Future?*

[100] Ian Haney Lopez for his book *Merge Left* conducted focus groups in which versions of this complaint were frequently heard. See also Arlie Russell Hochschild, *Strangers in Their Own Land* and Katherine J. Cramer, *The Politics of Resentment*.

[101] Katherine J. Cramer, *The Politics of Resentment: Rural Consciousness in Wisconsin and the Rise of Scott Walker* (Chicago: The University of Chicago Press, 2016), p. 223.

[102] Ian Haney Lopez, *Merge Left: Fusing Race and Class, Winning Elections, and Saving America* (New York: The New Press, 2019), p. 181.

[103] For a powerful indictment along these lines, see Thomas Frank's *Listen, Liberal, or What Ever Happened to the Party of the People?* (New York: Picador, 2016). The diversity within the top ranks of the Democratic Party is also misleading, in that it is racially diverse but not class diverse. Working class and poor people, of all colors, are not determining the Party's

priorities.

[104] As Frank Donoghue notes, new PhDs have internalized the idea that academia is a meritocracy, largely because their professors, administrators, academia at large, and the broader culture all enforce this. Thus, when many of us fail to land tenure track jobs, not only do we feel that we have personally failed, but that we have failed *intellectually*, which is supposed to be one of our strongest, indeed identity-defining traits. More broadly, in a winner-take-all culture it is impossible to think otherwise, because we laud the success stories with endless praise of their brilliance and talent while ignoring or stigmatizing the losers. For more, see Donoghue's excellent *The Last Professors*. William Deresiewicz also provides a compelling critique of the status-obsessed, winner-take-all culture found within elite universities circles in *Excellent Sheep: The Miseducation of the American Elite and the Way to a Meaningful Life.*

[105] As a thought experiment, imagine if a brilliant thinker like Charles Taylor wanted to write *A Secular Age*, or Sheldon Wolin *Politics and Vision,* as a young scholar. These masterpieces are the kind of work that takes years, even decades, of research and slow, subtle, thinking over time. This is nearly impossible in the academic climate today. You can't do it without tenure and if you have tenure you may be considered irrelevant and forgotten by the time you complete the study. It bears repeating: *this is a problem.*

[106] Frank Donoghue, *The Last Professors: The Corporate University and the Fate of the Humanities* (New York: Fordham University Press, 2008).

[107] For a brief summary of these problems see Randy Olson, *Houston, We Have a Narrative: Why Science Needs Story* (Chicago: The University of Chicago Press, 2015), pp. 8-12.

[108] Frank Donoghue, *The Last Professors.*

[109] Equivalent means similarly compensated and with similar levels of security and benefits.

[110] Sheldon Wolin, *The Presence of the Past* (Baltimore: The

Johns Hopkins University Press, 1989), p. 62.

[111] Jason Brennan and Phillip Magness, *Cracks in the Ivory Tower: The Moral Mess of Higher Education* (New York: Oxford University Press, 2019), p. 155.

[112] For a good discussion of how universities responded to surging college enrollment in the 1990s and 2000s by hiring more adjuncts (rather than tenure track professors), see Kevin Carey, "The Bleak Job Landscape of Adjunctopia for PhDs," *New York Times*, March 6, 2020.

[113] David Graeber, in his *Bullshit Jobs*, makes the case that in wealthy capitalist economies yearly income has something of an inverse relation with the social value of the work. For instance, the service workers who make the society run are the lowest paid, while senior figures in corporate bureaucracies receive the highest incomes. These figures may produce market value but it is not at all clear that they produce anything that serves the public good. Reflecting on the upside-down nature of American society, Howard Zinn opened a speech with "I start from the supposition that "the world is topsy-turvy, that things are all wrong, that the wrong people are in jail and the wrong people are out of jail, that the wrong people are in power and the wrong people are out of power." That pretty much sums it up. See "The Problem is Civil Obedience," Howard Zinn, November 1970, available at https://www.historyisaweapon.com/defcon1/zinnproblemobedience.html

[114] We can extend the author's logic in many darkly humorous ways: For instance, the fight for $15 is unnecessary. Most low-wage workers already make around $10 per hour and what's a few more? Surely not worth fighting for, right Brennan and Magness?

[115] Brennan and Magness don't give this advice but it is a plausible conclusion to draw from their claims.

[116] Sheldon Wolin, *The Presence of the Past* (Baltimore: The Johns Hopkins University Press, 1989), p. 50.

[117] Some strong contributions include Herb Childress, *The Adjunct Underclass*; Frank Donoghue, *The Last Professors*; and

Benjamin Ginsberg, *The Fall of the Faculty*. On a related note, William Deresiewicz in his *Excellent Sheep* offers a damning portrait of the obsession with prestige and credentialism found in America's elite universities.

[118] Sheldon Wolin, *The Presence of the Past* (Baltimore: The Johns Hopkins University, 1989), p. 26.

[119] Sheldon Wolin, *The Presence of the Past* (Baltimore: The Johns Hopkins University, 1989), p. 29.

[120] Many others have written impressively on this topic, including journalists like Naomi Klein.

[121] Sheldon Wolin, *The Presence of the Past* (Baltimore: The Johns Hopkins University, 1989), p. 31.

[122] See his *Climate Machines, Fascist Drives, and Truth* (Durham: Duke University Press, 2019), particularly chapter three.

[123] For one discussion of radical left political strategy, see Nick Srnicek and Alex Williams, *Inventing the Future* (New York: Verso Books, 2015).

[124] Romand Coles, *Visionary Pragmatism: Radical and Ecological Democracy in Neoliberal Times* (Durham: Duke University Press, 2016, p. 39.

[125] For thoughtful discussion of these points, see George Packer, *The Unwinding*, and Arlie Russell Hochschild, *Strangers in their own land*.

[126] This is documented powerfully in Arlie Russell Hochschild's *Strangers in their Own Land*. I myself have spent recent time as a maintenance worker ($12 per hour) and a meat and seafood worker in a grocery store ($9 per hour). These experiences have been deeply informative and have also profoundly impacted my sense of self.

[127] Daniel Markovits, *The Meritocracy Trap* (New York: Penguin Press, 2019), p. xiv.

[128] Sheldon S. Wolin and John H. Schaar, *The Berkeley Rebellion and Beyond: Essays on Politics and Education in the Technological Society*.

Printed in Great Britain
by Amazon